Cookies!

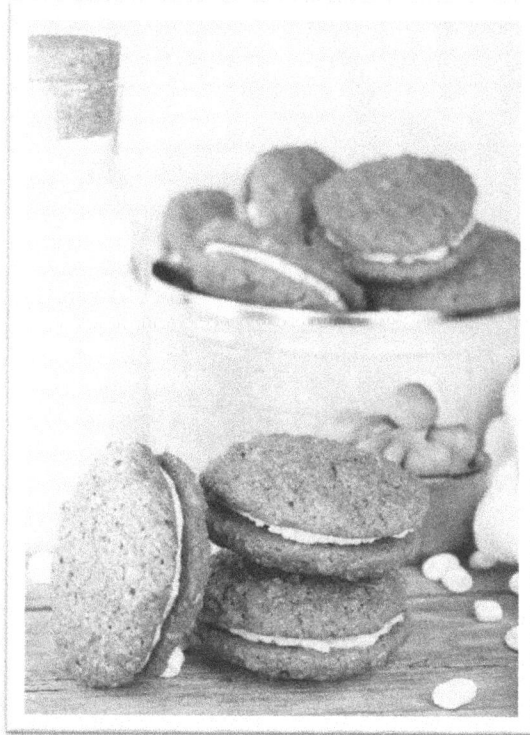

THE BEST COLLECTION OF
COOKIE RECIPES EVER
Just for YOU!

Nancy N. Wilson

PUBLISHER'S PAGE

COOKIES!

THE BEST COLLECTION OF COOKIE RECIPES EVER Just for YOU!

© Blurtigo Holdings, LLC
Published March 2020
United States of America

IMAGES

Chocolate Chip Cookies – Image by UMeimages@iStock

Chocolate Chip Squares – Image by Manyakotic@iStock

Christmas Cookies - Image by Blogmood @Pixabay

DEDICATION

To my daughter, Whitney,

who has become a master at making chocolate chip cookies
— her first cooking love!

and

To my granddaughter, Bella,

who learned to cook by my side, baking cookies.

Thank You

... for buying my book.
If you enjoy it, please take a minute and
post a review on Amazon and Goodreads or
any other platform where you purchased the book.

*For a complete list of my published cookbooks,
please, visit my Websites*

https://MamasLegacyCookcooks.com
https://NancyNWilson.com

Nancy N. Wilson

Please help me continuously improve my books.
If you find errors or omissions or have a problem with a recipe,
please, contact me immediately at wilsonemarketing@gmail.com
so I can make the necessary corrections.

TABLE OF CONTENTS

THE CLASSICS

BROWNIES, BARS, AND SQUARES

THE HOLIDAY COLLECTION

INTRODUCTION

Many young cooks are introduced to the kitchen through cookie making. It is an adventure of loving companionship, delightful aromas, and fresh delicious cookies from the oven that are shared by the entire family.

I have included a wide variety of cookies – including several versions of the American Classic Chocolate Chip Cookie – brownies, squares, and bars, plus traditional holiday treats.

There is likely a recipe in this cookbook that will satisfy your need for sweets.

Most of the recipes are made from scratch with a few that are made from mixes for a quick treat when you are working under a time crunch.

You will be well-prepared to make treats for your family during the holidays, for after school snacks, or just because love to bake.

I gained five pounds as I tested the newer recipes for you and hope you enjoy them as much as my neighbors (my taste-testers) and I did.

Keep your cookie jar full and enjoy every bite.

Love – from my kitchen to yours,

Nancy

COOKIE MAKING TOOLS

WELCOME!

Are you ready to make the best cookies ever?

You don't need many tools to make good cookies, but there are a few essential tools that will make you a better baker.

As with any project, when you have the right tools, the job is easier and the results are better.

Invest in the tools and enjoy cookie making to the fullest.

All of the items listed can be purchased easily through Amazon. Suggested brands with direct affiliate links are included for your convenience.

ESSENTIAL TOOLS

1. Lightweight Mixing Bowls - *Bellemain Lightweight Bowls with Covers* are an excellent choice! You'll be glad you have the covers.

2. Quality Measuring Cups and Spoons for Dry Ingredients
   The *Mykubi Stainless Steel* sets shown are good choices because they have more options than the standard sets. When you are ready to splurge, buy a 2nd set of each for convenience.

3. Three-Piece Pyrex Liquid Measuring cups – It is extremely useful to have all three sizes.

4. Bellmain Flour Sifter and/or OXO Good Grips Wire Whisk – You should have both of these in your kitchen. Either one will ensure that all ingredients are thoroughly mixed.

5. Brown Heavy-duty Wooden Mixing Spoons - If you have only one heavy-duty wooden spoon, this is the one to have. For a well-stocked baking kitchen, I recommend that you have at least three. Avoid the temptation to buy the cheaper, light-weight versions.

6. Electric Mixer
   This makes cookie baking easier and ensures all ingredients are evenly mixed. An electric mixer is a necessity if you bake cookies often. It will also keep your arms from turning to spaghetti noodle arms when beating the dough.

   Either a Kitchen Aid Stand Mixer or a VonShef Electric Hand Mixer (which I prefer and is much less expensive) will do the job.

7. Starpack Basics Silicone Flexible Spatulas
Nothing beats spatulas, especially if they are well-made and heavy-duty. You will use them every day for stirring and mixing, scraping the sides of bowls, spreading frosting, etc. – not just for cookie making. Avoid buying the ones with removable heads – they are too difficult to clean.

8. Set of 3 Cookie Scoops – These are extremely handy.

- The *large scoop* is the "ice cream" size – ideal for making BIG cookies, meatballs, pretty servings of mashed potatoes, and pouring correct portions of cupcake/muffin and pancake batter.

- The *medium scoop* makes perfectly-sized oatmeal and chocolate chip cookies, and sticky coconut macaroons.

- The *small scoop* is excellent for making tiny cookies, protein bites, truffles, and doubles as a melon baller.

9. USA Pan Half-Sheet Baking Pan - Cookie Sheets – Select these carefully. The type you use makes a huge difference in how the cookies turn out. Avoid dark metal pans or flimsy, inexpensive sheets. The above-recommended pan is **expensive but worth it!**

If you bake a lot of cookies, you will eventually want to purchase four of these – but two will work in the beginning. They have many uses in addition to baking cookies (sheet cakes, caramel corn, roasting vegetables, etc.).

10. Gridmann Pro Silicone Baking Mats (Set of Two) – 1 for each cookie sheet (11×16 inch size to fit your USA Pan cookie sheets). Reusable and dishwasher safe – and can be used for roasting fish, meat, potatoes, and veggies.

11. OXO Good Grips Silicone Cookie Spatula – This is the perfect size for transferring cookies from a pan to a wire cooling rack. It is heat resistant up to 600 degrees so it can be used for pan cooking, too. The flexible rubber coating makes it easy to scrape the dough off of spoons and bowls. It works like a rubber spatula and metal spatula in one!

12. Wilton Mega Wire Cooling Racks – It is preferable to have two cooling racks.

13. Faberware Classic Wood Rolling Pin
Necessary for shaped cookies. Rolling pins vary in price, but **an inexpensive wood rolling pin will last a long time.**

14. Cookie Cutters are basic for making Christmas cookies. It's worth it to buy quality cookie cutters. They should be strong, sturdy, and have sharp edges to give you a clean cut. We recommend you start with a good set of round cookie cutters that you can use for any occasion.

15. Air-tight Cookie Containers are important for storing cookies properly, to keep them fresh as possible. These Rubbermaid Takealongs are perfect for stacking several dozen cookies. Perfect for transporting, freezing, or keeping the cookies readily available for the family to enjoy. These come in a variety of sizes.

16. Oven Thermometers ensure that your oven temperature is correct. Most ovens are inaccurate and the variance can seriously affect the outcome of your cooking-baking efforts.

NON-ESSENTIAL TOOLS (Nice to Have)

1. OXO Food Scale for more accurate measuring. *(Not required, but a wise purchase - weighing is the most accurate way to measure.)* You will find many, many uses for this tool.

2. Cookie Press – It is simple to use, easy to clean, and the shapes are all pretty and fun.

3. Cookie Jar - When it comes to cookies, the taste is first, but the presentation is a close second. Make serving cookies fun. Kids and grandkids love to find cookies in the cookie jar.

4. Cupcake (or Cookie) Carrier – Make your life easier when traveling with cookies. The sides prevent the cookies from falling out when you remove the lid – nice!

COOKIE MAKING TIPS

BE A MASTER – USE THE RIGHT TOOLS!

If you want to be a master cookie maker, there are a few simple rules you must always follow. They are not difficult and make all the difference in your results.

Read the rules carefully and be prepared to implement them when you bake. It will be the beginning of a wonderful adventure as you consistently create delicious mouth-watering cookies to the delight of all your friends and family.

1. **Read the recipe carefully** so you don't make mistakes with your ingredients, measurements, and mixing process.

2. **Follow recipe directions exactly** – if you change things, the outcome may be different than you expected - and sometimes with disastrous results.

3. **Set out all of your equipment and ingredients** for easy access. Put each away as soon as you are finished with it (gives you more space to work).

4. **Use quality baking sheets** for the best cookies.
   - Choose cookies sheets carefully. Look for shiny aluminum sheets without sides so air can circulate and allow cookies to bake evenly.
   - Dark cookie sheets absorb more heat and make it difficult to control browning.
   - Insulated cookies sheets slow down baking and provide control, but require longer bake times.
   - Invest in wire cooling racks – they are critical for cooling cookies as quickly as possible. If you don't have wire racks – transfer the warm cookies to a chilled cookie sheet or cooled wooden cutting board lined with paper towels
   - Be sure to allow used cookie sheets to cool before you place freshly cut cookies on them for baking.
   - Prevent cookie dough from sticking to the cookie cutter by dipping the cutter into flour before each cut.
   - Cookie sheets should be at least two inches smaller than the inside of your oven so the heat can circulate.
   - Arrange the oven racks before you preheat the oven so the cookies can be baked in the center of the oven.
   - Always bake only one sheet of cookies at a time – on the center rack.

5. **Check your oven temperature** with an oven thermometer. They're inexpensive and will save you a million headaches. Most oven temps are inaccurate and can affect your baking results.

6. **Learn to measure ingredients correctly.**
   Dry Ingredients
   - **Spoon** flour or other light, powdery **dry ingredients** into your **measuring** cup or spoon until it makes a dome on the top.
   - Carefully level it off with the back of a knife. Be careful to NOT PACK the ingredient down.

   Liquid Ingredients
   - To measure liquids, place an appropriately sized liquid measuring cup on a flat, stable surface (don't hold it in your hand!).
   - Pour in your liquid until it is just under the line.

     - Squat or bend down so that your eye is exactly level with the top of the liquid.
     - Notice that the top surface of the liquid is not perfectly flat—it is slightly rounded with a top and a bottom. The rounded line is called a *meniscus*.
     - To measure liquid accurately, slowly add liquid until the *bottom* of the meniscus is perfectly level with the measuring line on the cup. (See image below.)

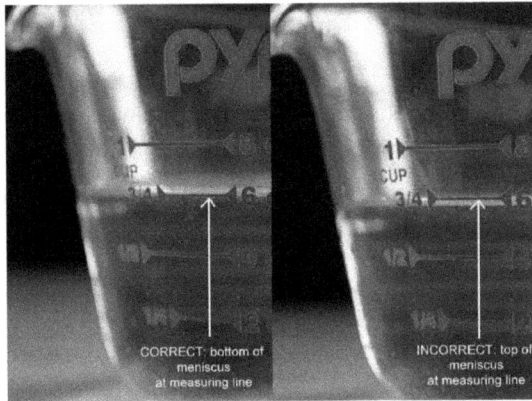

7. **If a recipe calls for room temperature ingredients, *use room temperature ingredients*.** If you don't, your cookies won't taste the way they should.

   If you forget to set out your butter and eggs to bring to room temp, try these tricks:

   Butter
   - Place measured butter in a microwave-safe bowl
   - Place 2 cups of water in a microwave-safe cup or bowl and heat to boiling (2-3 minutes).
   - Quickly remove water from microwave and replace with the butter, close the door and let it sit for 10 minutes to warm the butter to room temp.

Eggs

- Pace eggs in a cup or bowl and cover them with warm (not hot) tap water. Allow the eggs to sit in the water until they are no longer cool to the touch (5 to 10 minutes).

8. **Mix sugars and butter until creamy and fluffy.** It usually takes about 5 minutes at high speed to mix well. Don't shortcut this process.

9. **Sift dry ingredients** together before adding them to the butter/sugar mixture – or at least, whisk them together with a wire whisk until thoroughly mixed.

10. If the cookie dough is particularly sticky, wet, or greasy (or the recipe requires it), **chill the cookie dough**. Chilling cookie dough helps prevent spreading. The colder the dough, the less likely the cookies are to over-spread into greasy puddles.

11. **Use silicone baking mats** to prevent excessive spreading. They grip the bottom of the cookies and prevent spreading; they also promote even browning. If possible, avoid using nonstick spray or butter on the pans. Both create an overly greasy foundation, causing the cookies to spread too much.

12. **Use a cookie scoop** to place cookie dough on the baking sheets. This ensures equally-sized cookies in each batch for more even baking.

13. **Never place cookie dough on a hot baking sheet.** This is a BIG NO-NO! It's best to own a few extra cookie sheets so you always have a room temperature sheet on hand.

14. **Baking times in recipes are guidelines**. Use your own best judgment on how long to bake the cookies.

    Set the timer for the lower recommended time and then, keep a close eye. Look at the cookies themselves. The cookies are done when the edges are set and lightly browned.

    If you are making larger cookies that the recipes call for, you will have to increase the cooking time slightly (and a higher calorie count).

15. **Bake one batch of cookies at a time** for the best possible results. If you are in a time crunch and must bake more than one batch at a time, rotate the baking sheets from the top rack to bottom rack a couple of times through the baking process to encourage even browning.

    Baking more than one batch may also increase the cooking time slightly.

16. **When cookies are done**, remove from the oven and cool for 3 to 5 minutes on the baking sheet – then, **transfer to a wire cooling rack**. Cookies need air circulation while cooling to avoid soggy bottoms.

17. When cookies are completely cooled, **store in airtight containers at room temperature or freeze** for up to three months. Be sure to date and label freezing containers.

18. **When making frosting for decorating cookies:**
     - Beat softened butter with an electric mixer until smooth.
     - Add powdered sugar, vanilla, and milk and beat until smooth.
     - Add adding additional sugar or milk to reach desired consistency/
     - Frosting must be fairly stiff to work well when frosting cookies – avoid making it too thin.
     - Separate into small bowls and color as desired.
     - Frost cookies and top with assorted sprinkles.
     - If you do not want to decorate with frosting, sprinkle the cutout cookies with granulated or colored sugars before baking – then no frosting is required.

THE CLASSICS

ALMOND BISCOTTI

These almond biscotti are everything you expect in the perfect biscotti: buttery, lightly sweet, crunchy — and delicious any time of day!

48 Biscotti – 93 calories each

INGREDIENTS

- 2½ all-purpose flour, spooned into a measuring cup and leveled off with a knife
- ¼ cup cornmeal
- 1 teaspoon baking powder
- 1 teaspoon salt
- 1 teaspoon anise seeds, crushed with the back of a spoon into a powder
- 10 tablespoons unsalted butter
- 1 1/3 cup sugar
- 2 large eggs
- 2 teaspoons vanilla extract
- ½ teaspoon almond extract
- 1¾ cups slivered almonds, chopped finely

DIRECTIONS

1. *Set the oven racks in the upper and middle thirds of the oven and preheat the oven to 350° F.*

2. *Line two baking sheets with parchment paper.*

3. *In a medium bowl, whisk together the flour, cornmeal, baking powder, salt, and crushed anise seeds.*

4. *In a medium bowl, using a hand-held mixer, cream the butter and sugar until light and fluffy, about 2 minutes.*

5. *Add the eggs, one at a time, beating well after each addition and scraping down the bowl as necessary.*

6. *Mix in the vanilla and almond extracts.*

7. *Add the flour mixture and minced almonds; mix on low speed until just combined.*

8. Dust your hands lightly with flour and divide the dough into evenly into two balls.

9. Wrap the balls in plastic wrap and refrigerate for at least 15 minutes.

10. Remove the dough from the refrigerator and divide each disk into two equal pieces.

11. Dust your hands with flour and form each portion into logs about 2-inches wide and ¾-inch tall – place directly onto the lined baking sheets. Leave about 4 inches of space between the logs to allow the dough to spread. If the dough is sticky, dust your hands with more flour as necessary).

12. Bake for 25-30 minutes, rotating the pans from top to bottom and front to back midway through, until the loaves are firm to the touch and golden around the bottom edges.

13. Remove from the oven and let cool for 20 minutes.

14. When the logs are cool, transfer them to a cutting board.

15. Using a serrated knife and a sawing motion, cut the logs diagonally into generous ½" slices. (They will look a little undercooked in the middle.)

16. Arrange the cookies, cut side down, on one of the lined baking sheets. It will be a tight squeeze; it's not necessary to leave any space between the cookies.

17. Return the cookies to the oven on the middle rack and cook for 5-7 minutes, until lightly golden on the underside.

18. Remove the pan from the oven, carefully flip the biscotti over and cook for 5 minutes more, until lightly golden all over.

19. Let cool on the baking sheet completely before serving. The cookies will keep in an airtight container for up to a month.

RECIPE TIPS

To Freeze the Dough

- The dough can be frozen for up to 3 Months - shape the dough into 2 logs, wrap each securely in plastic wrap, and place them in a sealable bag.

- When ready to bake, remove the logs from the freezer, thaw the dough until pliable, and then proceed with recipe.

To Freeze after Baking

- *After the biscotti are completely cooled, double-wrap them securely with aluminum foil or plastic freezer wrap.*

- *Thaw overnight on the countertop before serving.*

- *You can also prep the biscotti through the first round of baking and cut them before freezing. (This allows you to do more of the work ahead, and because it will already be sliced, it will take less time to defrost and bake.)*

ALMOND MACAROONS

These rich, delicious cookies are perfect for homemade Christmas gifts. Drizzle with or dip in chocolate for an extra taste temptation.

30 Cookies – 45 calories each

INGREDIENTS

- 7 ounces almond paste
- 1 cup powdered sugar
- 1 pinch salt
- 3 large egg whites
- ½ teaspoon almond extract (optional)

DIRECTIONS

1. In a medium bowl, mix the almond paste, powdered sugar, and salt until finely crumbled.

2. Using a food processor or electric mixer slowly add the egg whites and almond extract, mixing until smooth – about 1 minute.

3. Scrape the mixture into a large, heavy saucepan and cook, stirring constantly, over medium heat until slightly thickened, about 4 minutes.

4. Remove from heat and pour into a bowl.

5. Refrigerate until cool and slightly firm - 20 to 30 minutes.

6. When the batter is almost ready, preheat the oven to 350° F.

7. Generously grease two cookie sheets.

8. Drop the batter by the heaping teaspoonful, onto the cookie sheet - allowing about 2 inches between cookies.

9. Bake - 1 sheet at a time, until the cookies are lightly tinged with brown - about 15 to 17 minutes.

10. Let stand for 1 or 2 minutes and place on a wire rack to cool.

11. For a finishing touch, drizzle with melted chocolate chips or dip the bottom in chocolate.

AMISH SUGAR COOKIES

You will want to make these cookies regularly and also share them with your friends and family. They are a great cookie choice for decorating during the holidays, wonderful for after-school snacks, and perfect for church buffets.

60 Cookies – 117 calories each

INGREDIENTS

- 1 cup butter (2 cubes), softened
- 1 cup vegetable oil
- 1 cup sugar
- 1 cup confectioners sugar
- 2 large eggs
- 1 teaspoon vanilla extract
- 4½ cups all-purpose flour
- 1 teaspoon baking soda
- 1 teaspoon cream of tartar

DIRECTIONS

1. *Preheat the oven to 375° F.*

2. *Set out two ungreased baking sheets.*

3. *In a large bowl, using an electric hand-held mixer, beat the butter, oil, and sugars together.*

4. *Add the eggs and beat until well blended.*

5. *Add the vanilla.*

6. *Whisk together the flour, baking soda, and cream of tartar; slowly stir into the creamed mixture.*

7. *Drop by small teaspoonfuls onto baking sheets.*

8. *Bake in the preheated oven until lightly browned, 8-10 minutes.*

9. *Remove to wire racks to cool.*

10. *They can be eaten plain, dusted with powdered sugar, or frosted.*

RECIPE TIPS

- *Use salted butter and a splash of almond extra for extra flavor.*

- *If you like sweeter cookies, add a pinch of granulated sugar on top of each cookie.*

BLACK AND WHITE COOKIES

These cookies are classic New York City. They are soft, pillow-like cookies with a thick layer of frosting, half chocolate and half vanilla – and they are supposed to be BIG! Of course, you can make them small if you choose, but that would be blasphemy to a native New Yorker.

24 Small Cookies – 194 calories each (can also make 12 large cookies)

INGREDIENTS

The Cookies

- 1¾ cups all-purpose flour
- ½ teaspoon baking powder
- ½ teaspoon baking soda
- 1/8 teaspoon salt
- 10 tablespoons butter, room temperature
- 1 cup granulated sugar
- 1 egg, room temperature
- 1 tablespoon vanilla extract
- 1/3 cup sour cream, room temperature

The Frosting

- 5 cups confectioners sugar
- 7 tablespoons whole milk, divided
- 2 tablespoons light corn syrup
- 1 teaspoon vanilla extract
- ½ teaspoon salt
- 3 tablespoons unsweetened cocoa powder

DIRECTIONS

Make the Cookies

1. Preheat oven to 350 °F.

2. Line two baking sheets with parchment paper.

3. Whisk together the flour, baking powder, baking soda, and salt in a small bowl; set aside.

4. Using a hand-held electric mixer, beat together the butter and sugar on medium-high speed, until light and fluffy, about 2 minutes.

5. Beat in the egg and vanilla, continuing to beat until well-combined, ~ 1 minute.

6. Reduce speed to low and add in half of the dry ingredients, followed by the sour cream, and ending with the rest of the dry ingredients.

7. Continue to beat on low until no streaks of flour remain.

8. To make New-York-style BIG cookies, grease a ¼ cup measuring cup to use as a scoop.

9. Scoop batter by ¼ cupsful and drop onto the prepared baking sheet.

10. Be sure cookies are 3-4 inches apart to allow for spreading.

11. Bake for 16 to 18 minutes, or until the edges of the cookies are lightly browned.

12. Cool cookies on the baking sheets for 5 minutes, then transfer to wire racks to cool completely before frosting.

Make the Frosting

13. Beat together the powdered sugar, 6 tablespoons of the milk, corn syrup vanilla extract, and salt.

14. Divide the frosting in half, moving half to another bowl.

15. Mix in the cocoa powder and the remaining 1 tablespoon of milk to one bowl.

16. Cut small sheets of wax paper and place over one-half of each cookie before frosting.

17. With a clean, dry knife, spread vanilla frosting onto the bottom of half of the cookie, overlapping on top of the wax paper.

18. Leave the wax paper in place and chill the frosted cookies in the refrigerator for 30 minutes, or until frosting is set.

19. Slowly pull up the wax paper. Frost the remaining half of the cookie with the chocolate frosting. Allow the frosting to set completely, ~ 1 hour.

RECIPE TIPS

- *Cookies can be stored up to 3 days in an airtight container at room temperature – or in the refrigerator for up to a week.*

- *If you need to stack the cookies, place a piece of wax paper between each layer of cookies to prevent them from sticking together.*

Chocolate Chip Cookies
Original Toll House® Recipe

This is the original Toll House® Cookie Recipe from the package. There are dozens of variations you may want to try, but this recipe always works! So, start here and enjoy every scrumptious bite.

60 Cookies – 108 Calories each

INGREDIENTS

- 2¼ cups all-purpose flour
- 1 teaspoon baking soda
- 1 teaspoon salt
- 1 cup (2 sticks) butter, softened
- ¾ cup granulated sugar
- ¾ cup packed brown sugar
- 1 teaspoon vanilla extract
- 2 large eggs
- 2 cups Nestlé® Toll House® Semi-Sweet Chocolate Morsels *(Experiment with different chocolates, butterscotch, or a mixture of different morsel flavors.)*
- 1 cup chopped nuts (optional)

DIRECTIONS

1. *Preheat oven to 375° F.*

2. *Generously butter two large cookie sheets.*

3. *Measure and place flour, baking soda, and salt in a small bowl – whisk together; set aside.*

4. *Place the softened butter, granulated sugar, brown sugar, and vanilla extract in a large mixing bowl and beat with a handheld electric mixer until creamy.*

5. *Add eggs, one at a time, beating well after each addition.*

6. *Gradually beat in the flour mixture – ½ cup at a time. Beat until well-blended, but don't over mix.*

7.   Using a wooden spoon, stir in the chocolate morsels and nuts.

8.   Use a cookie scoop or a large tablespoon and drop on cookie sheets about 2-3 inches apart.

9.   Bake for 9 to 11 minutes or until golden brown.

10. Cool on baking sheets for 2 minutes.

11. Using a pancake turner, remove cookies from pan and let cool on wire racks that have been covered with clean, dry paper towels.

12. Spoon up another batch on the cookie sheets and continue baking until all dough has been used.

RECIPE TIPS

- As soon as you remove the cookies from the oven, use two tablespoons to slightly scrunch up the edges. This creates a crispier edge and a softer, chewy center.

- Dough may be stored in the refrigerator for up to one week or in the freezer for up to eight weeks. Cook whenever the mood strikes you – one cookie sheet batch at a time.

VARIATIONS
Cookie Bars

1.   Preheat oven to 350° F.

2.   Butter a 15 X 10-inch jelly-roll pan.

3.   Prepare cookie dough exactly as described as above through Step 7.

4.   Then, spread the dough into a well-buttered pan and bake for 20 to 25 minutes until golden brown.

5.   Set the pan on a wire rack to cool.

6.   Cut into squares - makes 4 dozen bars.

This recipe is from www.VeryBestBaking.com. Nestlé® Toll House® is a registered trademark of Société des Produits Nestlé S.A., Vevey, Switzerland.

CHOCOLATE, CHOCOLATE CHIP COOKIES

If you are a chocoholic like a couple of my children, this is the cookie for you!

12 Large Cookies - 445 Calories each (can make 24 cookies for ½ the calories each)

INGREDIENTS

- 2 cups flour
- ½ cup unsweetened cocoa powder
- 1 teaspoon baking soda
- 1 teaspoon kosher salt
- 1 cup unsalted butter, softened
- 1 cup granulated sugar
- ½ cup packed light brown sugar
- 2 eggs
- 1 teaspoon vanilla extract
- 2 cups chocolate chips
  (Mixture of semi-sweet, milk, and white)

DIRECTIONS

1. Preheat oven to 350° F.

2. Prepare two baking sheets – line with parchment paper (or grease well).

3. Whisk together flour, cocoa powder, baking soda, and salt in a bowl; set aside.

4. In a large bowl, beat butter and sugars on medium speed of a hand mixer until fluffy, about 3 minutes.

5. Add eggs one at a time, beating well after each addition until smooth; beat in vanilla.

6. Add dry ingredients, and beat until just combined - Stir in chocolate chips.

7. Roll cookies into balls and place on baking sheets about 4-inches apart.

8. Refrigerate for 4 hours or up to overnight.

9.   Bake in the preheated oven, rotating once halfway through (about 15 minutes).

10.   Cool slightly before serving.

RECIPE TIPS

- *The dough is very soft and works best if refrigerated for at least 4 hours before baking. This makes the cookies thick and chewy.*

- *The dough can be frozen for several months, so stash a few in the freezer to bake anytime you are craving chocolate. Be sure to date the freezer bags.*

CHOCOLATE-DIPPED PEANUT BUTTER SANDWICH

This is the perfect after-school snack for the kids and their friends (and you too). The recipe requires only four ingredients and practically no time. You will be blown away.

15 Sandwich Cookies – 155 Calories each

INGREDIENTS

- ½ cup creamy peanut butter
- 30 round butter-flavored crackers (i.e., Ritz Crackers)
- 1 cup white, semisweet or milk chocolate chips
- 1 tablespoon shortening

DIRECTIONS

1. *Spread peanut butter on half of the cracker.*

2. *top with remaining crackers to make sandwiches.*

3. *Refrigerate until firm.*

4. *In a double boiler over simmering water or at 30-second intervals in a microwave, melt chocolate chips and shortening - stirring until smooth.*

5. *Dip sandwiches in chocolate mixture and allow excess to drip off.*

6. *Place on waxed paper; let stand until set.*

RECIPE TIPS

- *Do not omit the shortening. It helps the coating hold its shape.*

- *Dark chocolate chips not only taste good, they are better for you than milk chocolate.*

CHOCOLATE KISS COOKIES

These are wonderful holiday cookies, or a yummy anytime treat. The surprise chocolate centers will delight everyone!

25 Cookies – 103 calories each

INGREDIENTS

- 1½ cup all-purpose flour
- 1/8 teaspoon ground cinnamon
- ¾ cup butter (1½ cubes), softened (no substitutes)
- 1/3 cup light brown sugar, firmly packed
- 1½ teaspoons vanilla extract
- 25 solid Hershey's Kisses
- 1½ tablespoons powdered sugar
- ¾ teaspoon unsweetened cocoa powder

DIRECTIONS

1. Set out 2 cookie sheets - do not grease.

2. Preheat oven to 350° F.

3. Sift the flour and cinnamon together into a small mixing bowl and set aside.

4. In a medium-sized bowl, cream together the butter and brown sugar with an electric mixer set on high speed until light and fluffy.

5. Add the vanilla.

6. Stir in the flour ½ cup at a time, mixing thoroughly until well blended.

7. Make 1" balls and flatten into 2" rounds.

8. Place the rounds on the ungreased cookie sheets about 1 inch apart.

9. Set 1 chocolate kiss in the center of each round.

10. Close the dough around the kiss and seal it.

11. Bake for about 15 minutes - until golden brown.

12. While cookies are baking, combine the powdered sugar and cocoa in a small bowl.

13. When cookies are done, remove them from the oven and sprinkle the powdered sugar mixture over the hot cookies. (The best way to do this is to place the mixture in a strainer, saltshaker, or flour sifter.)

14. Cool on the cookie sheets for 10 minutes; then, transfer the cookies to wire racks to cool completely.

RECIPE TIPS

- Use different candy for the center. There are several varieties of Chocolate Kisses.

- Sprinkle with powdered sugar only (omit the cocoa).

Chocolate Orange Cookies

These soft, chewy chocolate cookies with a blend of orange and chocolate, topped with orange icing are exquisite. Every bite is a lovely treat.

14 Cookies – 152 calories each

INGREDIENTS

The Cookies

- 6 tablespoons butter, softened
- ½ cup granulated sugar
- Zest of 1 medium orange
- 1 egg, room temperature
- 1 teaspoon real vanilla extract
- 1 cup all-purpose flour
- ¼ cup Baker's® unsweetened cocoa powder
- 1 teaspoon baking powder
- ¼ teaspoon salt
- ¼ cup chopped walnuts
- ½ teaspoon cinnamon
- ¼ teaspoon allspice

The Frosting

- ½ cup powdered sugar
- 1 tablespoon freshly-squeezed orange juice
- 1 teaspoon orange zest
- 1 tablespoon melted butter
- 1 tablespoon cream cheese, softened
- 1 drop (only) almond extract

DIRECTIONS

Make the Cookies

1. *Preheat oven to 350° F.*

2. *Line a large baking sheet with parchment paper.*

3. In a medium bowl, whisk together flour, cocoa powder, baking powder, and salt; set aside

4. With a hand-held electric mixer, cream together the butter, sugar and orange zest – mix for ~ 1 minute until well combined.

5. Add the egg – turn the mixer to medium-low speed and beat until well combined.

6. Add the vanilla extract.

7. Add the dry ingredients to the mixture – beat on medium-low speed (beat only until combined – do not overmix.)

8. Scoop out dough with a cookie scoop and roll into balls.

9. Place on the baking sheet about 2 inches apart.

10. Slightly flatten cookies with the palm of your hand to ¼" thick. (Don't flatten if you prefer fat, fluffy cookies.)

11. Bake for 10-13 minutes until edges are golden brown.

12. Remove from oven - cool on baking sheet for a few minutes before transferring to a wire rack covered with paper towels to finish cooling.

Make the Frosting

1. In a medium bowl, mix the powdered sugar, orange juice, zest, melted butter, and softened cream cheese.

2. Add a single drop of almond extract (optional).

3. Frost the cookies and set on the wire rack to allow icing to harden.

4. Sprinkle with a little extra orange zest for garnish.

RECIPE TIPS

Freeze the Dough

- *Roll the cookie dough into balls and place them on a cookie sheet lined with parchment paper and place in the freezer for 30 minutes.*

- *When the cookie dough balls are firm, transfer them to a **freezer-safe bag** or air-tight container and freeze for up to 3 months. (Be sure to label and date the bag/container.)*

- *When ready to bake, thaw at room temperature while preheating the oven - flatten and bake cookies as directed in the recipe.*

Chocolate Sandwich Cookies

Make a double batch and freeze to keep on hand for after-school treats or a sweet treat with your coffee or tea. Make double-sized cookies and fill with ice cream for delicious ice cream sandwiches.

72 Cookies – 188 calories each cookie sandwich

INGREDIENTS

Cookies

- 2 packages Duncan Hines® Devil's Food Cake Mix (regular size)
- 1 cup canola oil
- 4 large eggs

Filling

- 8 ounces cream cheese, softened
- ¼ cup butter, softened
- 2½ cups powdered sugar
- 1 teaspoon vanilla extract

DIRECTIONS

Make the Cookies

1. *Preheat the oven to 350° F.*

2. *Set out two ungreased baking sheets.*

3. *In a large bowl, combine the cake mixes, eggs, and oil; roll into 1" balls - place 2" apart on ungreased baking sheets – do not flatten.*

4. *Bake at for 8-10 minutes or until set.*

5. *Cool for 5 minutes before removing to wire racks (cookies will flatten as they cool).*

Make the Filling

6. *In a small bowl, beat cream cheese and butter until fluffy.*

7. *Beat in sugar and vanilla until smooth.*

8. *Spread on the bottoms of half of the cookies; top with remaining cookies - store in the refrigerator.*

RECIPE TIPS

- *Freeze without the filling – thaw and add filling for another time.*

- *Substitute the cream cheese filling with ice cream for ice cream sandwiches.*

DOUBLE CHOCOLATE BUTTERSCOTCH CHIP COOKIES

This is a different, rich and buttery version of the traditional chocolate chip cookie that I think you will enjoy.

20 Cookies – 352 calories each

INGREDIENTS

- 1 cup of butter (2 cubes), softened
- 1¾ cups granulated sugar
- 2 eggs
- 2 teaspoon vanilla (or brandy)
- 1 oz. unsweetened baking chocolate, melted
- ¼ cup sour cream
- 2 cups flour
- ¾ cup cocoa
- ½ teaspoon baking soda
- ½ teaspoon salt
- ¼ teaspoon baking powder
- 2 cups butterscotch chips (or white chocolate chips)
- 1 cup chopped pecans

DIRECTIONS

1. *Preheat the oven to 350° F.*

2. *Set out two buttered cookie sheets (or lined with parchment paper).*

3. *In a medium bowl, whisk the dry ingredients together until well mixed.*

4. *Mix the butter and sugar until light and fluffy in a large bowl, using an electric hand-held mixer.*

5. *Add the eggs one at a time, and beat well after each addition.*

6. *Add the vanilla or brandy.*

7. *Carefully melt the chocolate in a medium microwave-safe bowl - heating at 30-second intervals.* (As the chocolate begins to lose its shape, remove from the microwave and stir (be careful – the chocolate scorches easily).

8. *Stir in the sour cream.*

9. *Stir into the egg and sugar mixture.*

10. *Using a low speed on the mixer, add the dry ingredients to the chocolate mix (a cup at a time).*

11. *Mix until everything is well-blended.*

12. *Stir in the chocolate chips and the nuts.*

13. *Using a small cookie scoop (or tablespoon), drop dough onto prepared cookie sheets*

14. *Bake for 12-15 minutes.* (I cook 12 cookies on a large cookie sheet for 15 minutes and they are perfect.)

15. *Cool on the baking sheet for about five minutes, then move to a wire rack covered with a paper towel to finish cooling.*

16. *Store in an airtight container.*

RECIPE TIPS

- *Cookies spread very little –the size you drop is the size they finish.*

- *Because the cookies are so rich, we recommend keeping them small.*

Adapted from Betty Ford's Thanksgiving Double Chocolate Cookies

FROSTED CREAM CHEESE COOKIES

These soft, sweet, creamy cookies will mouth in your mouth. Every bite is perfection. A wonderful choice for afternoon coffee with friends. (And, a tasty indulgence for breakfast!)

24 Cookies – 107 calories each

INGREDIENTS

Cookies
- 7 tablespoons unsalted butter, softened
- 5 ounces full fat cream cheese – 4 oz. room temperature/1 oz. frozen
- ½ teaspoon salt
- 1 teaspoon cornstarch
- 1 cup powdered sugar
- 1 egg yolk
- 1¾ cup all-purpose flour

Frosting
- 1 egg white
- 1 cup powdered sugar
- ¼ teaspoon pure vanilla extract
- Water as needed
- Sprinkles, chocolate shavings, etc., as desired

DIRECTIONS

Make the Cookies

1. Using an electric mixer in a large bowl, combine the butter, vanilla, 4 ounces of cream cheese, salt and cornstarch until creamy (about 1 minute)

2. Add powdered sugar and flour, and combine until they form a dough.

3. Add egg yolk and combine just until it's mixed in.

4. Remove cream cheese from the freezer and cut into 1/4" cubes.

5. Stir the cubes into the dough using a spatula.

6.   Chill dough in the refrigerator for 1 hour.

7.   Preheat oven to 350° F.

8.   Set out cookie sheets lined with parchment paper.

9.   Roll the dough into 1" balls, and space evenly on the baking sheet.

10.   Press the tops of the dough to flatten into round discs.

11.   Bake until lightly golden (but not brown), ~18 minutes.

12.   Allow to cool on cookie sheet for 5 minutes – then, transfer to a wire rack.

Make the Frosting

1.   Meanwhile, use an electric mixer to beat the egg white and vanilla until frothy.

2.   Add powdered sugar and beat to glossy peak consistency, ~ 5-7 minutes.

3.   If the icing is too "thick" to spread, add 1 teaspoon of water at a time until it reaches a spreadable consistency.

Frost the Cookies

1.   Set out your sprinkle/chocolate shavings, if using.

2.   When cookies are completely cool, frost the cookies.

3.   Immediately add the sprinkles/chocolate shavings.

4.   Allow icing the harden slightly before serving, and enjoy!

GRAHAM CRACKER NO-BAKE COOKIES

This is the perfect starter recipe for making cookies with your children, as long as they are well supervised. They will be very proud of the finished product. Try it with chocolate too. (See the "Recipe Tips")

16 Cookies – 278 calories each

INGREDIENTS

- 9 graham cracker squares, whole
- 1 cup graham cracker crumbs
- 1 cup butter (2 cubes) - no substitutes
- 1 cup sugar
- 1 cup chopped nuts (walnuts or pecans)
- 1 cup coconut flakes

DIRECTIONS

1. *Line an 8" square baking pan with whole graham crackers.*

2. *Place more crackers in a large plastic freezer bag and crush with a rolling pin until you have 1 cup of crumbs; chop the nuts.*

3. *Melt the butter in a medium-sized saucepan; add the sugar, graham cracker crumbs, nuts, and coconut to the butter.*

4. *Bring to a boil over medium heat and boil for 30 seconds.*

5. *Pour over graham crackers in the pan and chill; cut in 2" squares and serve.*

RECIPE TIPS

- *Chill the cookies for an hour and top with a half recipe of the Chocolate Topping from Mississippi Mud Bars.*

Lemon Snowball Cookies

Even though I am a hard-core "cook from scratch" person, I make an exception for this recipe. With four simple ingredients, you can whip up these delightful cookies and impress your guests with your culinary skills.

66 Cookies – 37 calories each

INGREDIENTS

- 1 package lemon cake mix (regular size)
- 2¼ cups whipped topping
- 1 large egg
- Powdered sugar

DIRECTIONS

1. *Preheat the oven to 350° F.*

2. *Set out two ungreased baking sheets.*

3. *In a large bowl using a hand-held electric mixer, combine the cake mix, whipped topping and egg until well blended. (Batter will be very sticky.)*

4. *Drop by teaspoonfuls into confectioners sugar; roll lightly to coat.*

5. *Place on ungreased baking sheets and bake in preheated oven for 10-12 minutes or until lightly browned and tops are cracked.*

6. *Remove to wire racks to cool.*

Maple Syrup Chocolate Chip Cookies

This unusual chocolate chip cookie is crazy addictive. Eat one, and you want another. Its crispy, crunchy goodness will make it an instant favorite. You may never want to make chocolate chip cookies any other way once you have tried this recipe.

48 cookies – 223 calories each

INGREDIENTS

- 1 cup unsalted butter (2 cubes)
- 1½ cups light brown sugar, packed
- ½ cup granulated sugar
- 2 large eggs, room temperature
- 1 teaspoon pure vanilla extract
- ¼ cup real Vermont maple syrup
- 3¼ cups all-purpose white flour
- 2 teaspoons cornstarch
- 1 teaspoon baking powder
- 1 teaspoon baking soda
- 1 teaspoon salt
- 2 cups Nestle® Semi-sweet Chocolate Chips
  (A mixture of dark chocolate and milk chocolate also works well)

DIRECTIONS

1. Melt the butter and cool for at least 5 minutes.

2. While butter is cooling, whisk together the flour, cornstarch, baking powder, baking soda, and salt; set aside.

3. Place both sugars and cooled melted butter in a large bowl and mix with an electric hand-held mixer until well blended.

4. Add room temperature eggs, one at a time, mixing well after each.

5. Beat in the vanilla extract and maple syrup.

6. Gradually add the flour mixture to the mixture, beating well until all ingredients are blended.

7. Stir in the chocolate chips.

8. Cover the bowl with foil or Saran Wrap and refrigerate overnight (must chill for at least 60 minutes).

9. When ready to bake, preheat the oven the 350° F.

10. Set out two large cookie sheets and line with parchment paper (or cookies can be baked on an ungreased cookie sheet).

11. Drop one cookie scoop of dough onto the prepared cookie sheet – at least 2" apart.

12. Bake for 13 minutes – or until cookie is brown all over.

13. Allow cookies to cool slightly then remove to wire racks covered with paper towels to cool completely.

14. Store in a sealed plastic bag or air-tight container.

NOTE: Keep unbaked cookie dough in the fridge while waiting to cook the next batch – and SO NOT drop cookie dough onto a hot cookie sheet.

RECIPE TIPS

- Be sure the butter has cooled before mixing or the dough will be the wrong consistency. When melting the butter, heat in 30-second increments – don't let it bubble.

Mom's Favorite Molasses Cookies

My mother made these cookies without a recipe, so I had to find one that was as similar as I could remember. This is it! I hope you love the soft, chewy exquisite flavor as much as I do. There is no better treat than two of these cookies and a big glass of cold milk.

24 Cookies – 260 calories each

INGREDIENTS

- 1¼ cups softened butter (NOT melted)
- 2 cups sugar
- ½ cup molasses
- 2 eggs
- 4 cups flour
- 3 teaspoons baking soda
- 2 teaspoons cinnamon
- 1½ teaspoons ground cloves
- 1 teaspoon ginger
- ¼ teaspoon salt
- ¼ cup granulated sugar

DIRECTIONS

1. In a large bowl using a hand-held electric mixer, combine butter, sugar, molasses, and eggs – beat until smooth.

2. In a separate bowl, whisk together flour, baking soda, cinnamon, cloves, ginger, and salt.

3. Add flour mixture to wet ingredients and beat until all ingredients are thoroughly combined.

4. Refrigerate dough for at least 60 minutes.

5. Preheat oven to 350° F.

6. Grease cookie sheets or line with parchment paper.

7. Form dough into walnut-sized balls and roll tops in granulated sugar.

8. Place balls two inches apart on the cookie sheet, and flatten slightly.

9. Bake 9-12 minutes in the preheated oven. (For a soft, chewy cookie, remove from the oven at 9 minutes. For a crispier cookie, similar to a ginger snap, bake for the longer time.)

NEW YORK CHEESECAKE COOKIES

Who doesn't love cheesecake? Now you can enjoy a taste of New York in a cookie – a delightful blend of flavors that can be enjoyed anywhere, any time.

24 Cookies – 101 calories each

INGREDIENTS

- 1¼ cup graham crackers, finely crushed (1 sleeve)
- 1 cup flour
- 1½ teaspoon baking powder
- ½ cup (1 stick) unsalted butter, softened
- ½ cup brown sugar, packed
- 1 egg, separated
- 3 oz. cream cheese, softened
- ¼ cup granulated sugar
- ½ teaspoon lemon zest
- ½ teaspoon vanilla extract

DIRECTIONS

1. *Preheat the oven to 350° F.*

2. *Set out a non-stick or parchment-lined baking sheet.*

3. *In a large bowl, stir together the graham cracker crumbs, flour, and baking powder.*

4. *In a medium bowl, beat together the butter with the brown sugar using an electric hand mixer.*

5. *Add the egg white and beat until well combined.*

6. *Add to the graham cracker crumbs and blend until just combined.*

7. *In a separate medium bowl, beat together the softened cream cheese with the granulated sugar, egg yolk, lemon zest, and vanilla until well combined; set aside.*

8. *Using a small ice cream scoop, scoop out the cookie dough on the baking sheet. (If you do not have an ice scoop, then measure out the dough into scoops of about 2 tablespoons.)*

9. Flatten slightly, pressing your thumb in the center of the ball to create a small bowl shape.

10. Repeat with the remaining dough. Spoon the cream cheese into the indents in the cookies.

11. Bake until the filling is barely set and the cookies are lightly golden, ~12 minutes.

12. Allow to cool 5 minutes on the baking sheets before removing them – cool completely on a wire rack.

OATMEAL CHOCOLATE CHIP COOKIES

This is a version of one of the most famous chocolate chips-oatmeal cookies around (sorry I can't tell you which one), but now you can make them your own! Your children, spouse, and friends will love you for it. ENJOY!

48 Cookies – 387 calories each

INGREDIENTS

- 2 cups sugar
- 2 cups brown sugar, packed
- 1 pound real butter (4 cubes), softened
- 4 large eggs
- 2 tablespoons vanilla extract
- 4 cups flour
- 5 cups oatmeal
- 1 teaspoon salt
- 2 teaspoons baking powder
- 2 teaspoons baking soda
- 24 ounces chocolate chips (2 large packages)
- 8 ounces dark chocolate bar, grated
- 3 cups nuts (optional)

DIRECTIONS

1. *Preheat oven to 375° F.*

2. *Set out an ungreased cookie sheet.*

3. *Cream softened butter and both sugars together until fluffy,*

4. *Add vanilla – then, eggs one at a time, mixing well after each addition.*

5. *Sift in dry ingredients and mix well – the dough will be very stiff.*

6. *Stir in chocolate chips, grated chocolate bar, and nuts.*

7. *Drop by heaping tablespoonsful onto the ungreased baking sheet.*

8. *Bake in preheated oven 6 to 8 minutes (should look slightly undercooked).*

9. *Cool on a wire rack - If not eaten immediately, store in air-tight contain*

OATMEAL RAISIN COOKIES

This is my favorite cookie, and this is the best recipe for making them.

42 Cookies – 73 calories each

INGREDIENTS

- 1½ cups all-purpose flour
- 1 teaspoon baking powder
- ¼ teaspoon salt
- 1 cup light brown sugar, firmly packed
- ¾ cup butter (1½ cubes), softened (no substitutes)
- 2 large eggs
- 1 teaspoon vanilla extract
- 1½ cups rolled oats (regular or quick-cooking)
- 1 cup raisins

DIRECTIONS

1. *Preheat oven to 350° F.*

2. *Butter or grease 2 or 3 cookie sheets.*

3. *Sift the flour, baking powder, and salt together into a mixing bowl and set aside.*

4. *Cream the butter and sugar together with an electric mixer on high speed until light and fluffy.*

5. *Add vanilla and eggs one at a time, mixing thoroughly after each addition until smooth.*

6. *Add the flour in three portions and mix until thoroughly blended. When the mixture becomes too thick for the mixer, use a sturdy wooden spoon to continue.*

7. *Add the oats and raisins - mix well.*

8. *Drop the dough by rounded tablespoons onto the cookie sheets - keeping the cookies 2 inches apart.*

9. *Flatten each cookie slightly.*

10. *Bake for 10 to 12 minutes until lightly browned.*

11. Remove from oven and cool on the cookie sheet for 1 to 2 minutes.

12. Transfer cookies to a wire rack covered with a paper towel to cool completely. (Using a large pancake spatula will help prevent the cookies from breaking.)

RECIPE TIPS

- The cookies will keep for up to 5 days when stored in an airtight container.

- If the cookies become too soft, place them on a baking sheet and bake for 5 minutes at 300° F.

- This is a great way to serve hot cookies fresh from the oven every day.

OLD-FASHIONED PEANUT BUTTER COOKIES

This is a classic recipe with two variations from Betty Crocker Cookbook: 1500 Recipes for the Way You Cook Today (Wiley). You can use creamy or chunky peanut butter – all that changes is the texture. Variations are noted below in the "Recipe Tips" section.

30 Cookies – 110 calories each

INGREDIENTS

- ½ cup granulated sugar
- ½ cup packed brown sugar
- ½ cup peanut butter
- ½ cup butter, softened
- 1 egg
- 1¼ cups all-purpose flour
- ¾ teaspoon baking soda
- ½ teaspoon baking powder
- ¼ teaspoon salt
- Additional granulated sugar for sprinkling

DIRECTIONS

1. Heat oven to 375° F.

2. Whisk together the flour, baking soda, baking powder, and salt; set aside.

3. In a large bowl, beat together ½ cup granulated sugar, the brown sugar, peanut butter, butter, and egg with electric mixer on medium speed, or mix with a spoon, until well blended.

4. Add dry ingredients to the mixture until well-mixed.

5. Scoop and roll dough into 1¼" balls and place on cookie sheets, about 3 inches apart.

6. Flatten in crisscross pattern with fork dipped in additional granulated sugar.

7. Bake 9 to 10 minutes or until light brown - Cool 5 minutes

8. Remove from cookie sheets to wire racks covered with paper towels.

9.   *Store in airtight containers in layers separated by waxed paper.*

RECIPE TIPS
- *They can be kept at room temperature for up to 3 days or freeze for up to 3 months.*

VARIATIONS:

Rich Peanut Butter Chip Cookies
- Omit ½ cup granulated sugar
- Increase brown sugar to 1 cup.
- After adding the flour mixture, stir in 1 cup peanut butter chips.
- Shape dough into balls as directed.
- Dip tops of balls into granulated sugar, but do not flatten.
- Bake as directed.

Triple Surprise Cookies
- After adding the flour mixture 1⁄3 cup each
  - peanut butter chips
  - white vanilla baking chips
  - semisweet chocolate chips.
- Bake as directed. (Makes 30 cookies)

PEANUT BUTTER
CHOCOLATE CHIP COOKIES

Everyone will love this classic cookie combination of peanut butter and chocolate!

42 Cookies – 133 calories each

INGREDIENTS

- 1½ cups all-purpose flour
- 1 teaspoon baking soda
- 1 cup real butter (2 cubes)
- ½ cup creamy peanut butter
- ½ cup sugar
- ½ cup brown sugar, firmly packed
- 1 teaspoon vanilla extract
- 1 large egg - unbeaten (room temp)
- 1 ¾ cups (11.5-ounce package) milk chocolate chips
- 1 tablespoon granulated sugar to sprinkle on top of cookies

DIRECTIONS

1. Set out 2 or 3 cookie sheets - do not grease.

2. Preheat oven to 375° F.

3. Sift flour and baking soda into a small bowl and set aside.

4. Place the butter, peanut butter, both sugars, and vanilla extract in a large mixing bowl.

5. Using an electric hand-held mixer on high speed, beat until creamy.

6. Beat in the egg.

7. Gradually add the flour mixture - ½ cup at a time - blend thoroughly.

8. Stir in the chocolate chips.

9. Drop dough by rounded tablespoons onto cookie sheets.

10. Flatten slightly with a fork (to make the traditional peanut butter mark).

11. *Lightly sprinkle each cookie with granulated sugar.*

12. *Bake for 9 to 10 minutes or until edges are set, but centers are still soft.*

13. *Remove from oven and let cool on baking sheet for 2 or 3 minutes - then transfer to wire racks to cool completely. (A large pancake spatula works best for this purpose.)*

PECAN SANDIES

These cookies have several names. Some call them Mexican Wedding Cookies, others call them Snowball Cookies, which is a good name when making them for the holidays or to serve as a family snack with hot chocolate in front of a warm flickering fire. Whatever you call them, they will be a family favorite.

66 Cookies – 120 calories each

INGREDIENTS

- 1 cup cold salted butter, cut into chunks
- 1¾ cups powdered sugar
- 2 cups flour
- 1 teaspoon pure vanilla extract
- 1 cup finely ground pecans

DIRECTIONS

1. *Preheat the oven to 325° F.*

2. *Line a cookie sheet with parchment paper.*

3. *Cream together ¾ cup of the powdered sugar and butter.*

4. *Add the flour, vanilla, and ground pecans – stir until thoroughly blended.*

5. *Use a cookie scoop and shape dough into balls.*

6. *Place 2" apart on a prepared cookie sheet.*

7. *Bake until the edges turn gold, ~ 20 minutes.*

8. *Place cookies on a wire rack covered with paper towels to cool.*

RECIPE TIPS

To Store

- *Freeze in an airtight container, with wax paper between each layer for up to 6 months. Defrost 30 minutes.*

- *Just before serving, place the remaining cup of powdered sugar in a plastic bag. Add several cookies and shake gently to dust with sugar. Repeat until all cookies are dusted.*

RED VELVET
WHITE CHOCOLATE CHIP COOKIES

Soft red velvet white chocolate chip cookies made from scratch. Be sure to chill the dough for at least an hour. Be adventurous and substitute semi-sweet morsels for the white chocolate – or frost with white cream cheese frosting. They are delicious either way.

24 Cookies – 256 calories each

INGREDIENTS

- 2½ cups flour
- ½ cup unsweetened cocoa powder
- 1 teaspoon baking soda
- ¼ teaspoon salt
- 1 cup (2 sticks) salted butter, softened
- 1 cup granulated sugar
- 2/3 cup firmly packed light brown sugar
- 2 eggs
- 2 teaspoons red food coloring.
- 2 teaspoons pure vanilla extract
- 1 package (12 ounces) white or semi-sweet chocolate chips

DIRECTIONS

1. *Preheat oven to 350° F.*

2. *Line a large cookie sheet with parchment paper or spray with cooking spray.*

3. *Whisk together in a medium bowl the flour, cocoa powder, baking soda, and salt; set aside.*

4. *In a large bowl, beat together with a hand-held electric mixer both sugars and butter until light and fluffy.*

5. *Add eggs, food coloring, and vanilla – mix well.*

6. *Reduce mixer speed to low and slowly add flour mixture until well blended.*

7. *Stir in chocolate chips.*

8. *Using a cookie scoop, drop onto cookie sheet about 2" apart.*

9.   *Bake 8 to 10 minutes or until cookies are set.*

10.   *Place a few chocolate chips into the tops of the warm cookies (optional – for looks only). Or – when cooled completely, frost with white cream cheese frosting.*

11.   *Cool on cookie sheets (~1 minute) and remove to wire racks covered with paper towels to cool completely.*

RECIPE TIPS

- Use **Hershey's Cookies and Cream Chips** instead of white or semi-sweet chocolate chips.

Storing

- Store at room temperature for up to 1 week in an airtight container.

- Baked cookies freeze well for up to 3 months.

SALTED CHOCOLATE CHUNK COOKIES

This is a wonderful twist on an American Classic – which may very well become your first choice. You can make a double recipe, bake a batch for right now and freeze the dough for easy snacks whenever the cookie craving hits.

24 Cookies – 128 calories each (Recipe can be doubled)

INGREDIENTS

- ½ up (1 cube) unsalted butter, softened
- 2 tablespoons granulated sugar
- 2 tablespoons turbinado sugar (raw sugar)
- ¾ cup plus 2 tablespoons packed **dark brown** sugar
- **1 egg at room temperature**
- 1¾ cups all-purpose flour
- ¾ teaspoon baking soda
- ½ teaspoon kosher salt
- 6 ounces bittersweet chocolate (use high-quality chocolate), cut into ½" chunks with a serrated knife
- Maldon® Flaky salt for topping

DIRECTIONS

1. *In a small bowl, whisk the flour, baking soda, and salt to combine; set aside.*

2. *In a large bowl using a hand-held electric mixer on medium speed, cream together the butter and three sugars until light in color and fluffy – at least 5 minutes. Scrape the sides of the bowl often with a rubber spatula.*

3. *Beat in the egg and vanilla until well-combined – scraping the sides with a rubber spatula as you mix.*

4. *With the mixer on low, slowly add the prepared flour mixture ½ cup at a time. Mix only until streaks of flour still run throughout.*

5. *Add the chocolate and stir until everything comes together. DO NOT OVERMIX!*

6. *Finish mixing the dough by hand, taking care to scrape the sides and the bottom of the bowl to ensure ingredients are evenly distributed.*

7. **(Don't skip this step!)** Refrigerate the dough for 24 hours. This allows the flavors to intensify and improves the cookie texture when baked.

8. When ready to bake, preheat the oven to 360° F.

9. Line two baking sheets with parchment paper.

10. With a cookie scoop, place the dough onto the baking sheets.

11. Top the cookies with a pinch of flaky salt just before baking. You can also add another pinch immediately after baking for a nice finishing touch.

12. Bake for 10 to 12 minutes – until lightly golden on the outside but still gooey on the inside. DON'T OVER BAKE!

13. Cool on the baking sheets for at least 5 minutes or the cookies may fall apart.

14. Then, transfer to a wire rack covered with a paper towel to finish cooling.

15. These the most delicious the day of baking but will keep in a tightly sealed container for up to 2 days.

RECIPE TIPS

- Use all three sugars; additional dark brown sugar can be substituted for the turbinado sugar (also known as raw sugar).

- Chocolate chips can be used, but they won't puddle and melt into chocolate layers. You can also use a combination of a quality chocolate bar and chocolate chips.

- Roll unused dough into a 2-inch-thick log, wrap in parchment paper, and refrigerate for 1 week or freeze for up to 1 month. When you need a cookie fix, pull out the log, slice off two or three cookies and bake. YUM!

- Baked cookies can also be frozen.

SIMPLE BUTTERY
SHORTBREAD COOKIES

These are delightful, "melt-in-your-mouth" buttery cookies that finish with a nice crunch when lightly sprinkled with granulated sugar while they're hot. It is also the perfect cookie to bake and decorate for any holiday – including Halloween. It is an excellent choice to make with the little ones or for your teenagers to try their hand at holiday baking.

36 Cookies – 36 calories each

INGREDIENTS

- 1 cup (2 sticks) unsalted butter, chilled and cut into ½" cubes
- ½ cup superfine sugar, plus additional for sprinkling
- ½ teaspoon pure vanilla extract
- Zest of half a lemon
- 1 2/3 cups (8 ounces) unbleached flour
- 4 teaspoons granulated sugar, for sprinkling

DIRECTIONS

1. *Preheat the oven to 350° F.*

2. *Line two cookie sheets with parchment paper.*

3. *In a large bowl, using a hand-held electric mixer, beat the butter, sugar, vanilla, and lemon zest on medium speed until fluffy and lemony-yellow in color, ~ 2 minutes.*

4. *With the mixer on very low speed, gradually add the flour, mixing until the dough is soft and pliable. Do not overmix.*

5. *Gather the dough into a ball.*

6. *Place the dough on a lightly floured flat work surface and sprinkle the top with flour and roll into a ½" thick rectangle.*

7. *Place on a large sheet of plastic wrap. Fold the plastic wrap loosely over the dough to enclose it, keeping the edges of the wrap at the right angles.*

8. *Using a rolling pin, roll the dough to fill the corners of the wrap. (This will give you a nice rectangle that will be easy to roll out after chilling.)*

9. Transfer to a baking sheet and refrigerate until the dough is chilled and firm, but not rock hard, ~ 1 hour.

10. Position the racks in the top third of the preheated oven.

11. Rap the four edges of the dough rectangle a few times on the work surface.

12. Unwrap the dough and place it on a lightly floured work surface.

13. Sprinkle the top of the dough with flour.

14. Roll out the dough into a ¼"-inch thick rectangle. (If the dough cracks, it is too cold. Let stand at room temperature for 5 to 10 minutes and try again.)

15. Using a 2-inch round cookie cutter dipped in flour, cut out the shortbread, cut cookies close together to reduce the number of scraps.

16. Transfer the cookies to the prepared baking sheets, leave about ½- inch space between the cookies.

17. Gather up the dough, rewrap in plastic, roll into another ¼-inch thick rectangle, chill for about 10 minutes, and cut out more cookies.

18. Repeat chilling and cutting until all the dough is cut out.

19. Bake, switching the position of the sheets from top to bottom and front to back halfway through baking, until the shortbread is very lightly browned, 10 to 12 minutes.

20. Remove from the oven and immediately sprinkle the cookies with the granulated sugar (the sugar will not stick if the cookies aren't hot).

21. Cool the cookies completely on the baking sheets.

SNICKERDOODLES

These are an "old-fashioned" favorite cookie that must be in the repertoire of any good cookie-maker. They are easy to make and are a delightful treat for friends and family.

~48 cookies – 82 calories each

INGREDIENTS

- 1 cup butter, softened
- 1½ cups sugar
- 1 teaspoon baking soda
- 1 teaspoon cream of tartar
- ¼ teaspoon salt
- 2 eggs
- 1 teaspoon vanilla
- 3 cups all-purpose flour
- ¼ cup sugar
- 2 teaspoons ground cinnamon

DIRECTIONS

1. Preheat the oven to 375° F.

2. Combine ¼ cup sugar and cinnamon in a small bowl; set aside.

3. In a large mixing bowl beat butter with an electric mixer on medium to high speed for 30 seconds.

4. Add 1½ cups sugar, baking soda, cream of tartar, and salt.

5. Beat until combined, scraping sides of bowl occasionally.

6. Mix in eggs and vanilla until combined.

7. Mix in as much of the flour as you can with the mixer.

8. Then, stir in any remaining flour with a wooden spoon.

9. Cover and chill dough about 1 hour or until easy to handle.

10. Roll balls in cinnamon-sugar mixture to coat.

11.   *Place 2 inches apart on an ungreased cookie sheet.*

12.   *Bake for 10 to 12 minutes or until bottoms are light brown.*

13.   *Transfer cookies to a wire rack; cool before serving.*

SNICKERDOODLE CRISPS

Snickerdoodles can be made soft or crunchy. Above is the soft version, but you may also want to try this crispy, cinnamon, ginger, and nutmeg version for a different version of perfection.

~5 dozen – 84 calories each

INGREDIENTS
- 1 cup butter, softened
- 2 cups sugar
- 2 large eggs
- 2 teaspoons vanilla extract
- 3 cups all-purpose flour
- 4 teaspoons ground cinnamon
- 2 teaspoons ground ginger
- ¾ teaspoon ground nutmeg
- ½ teaspoon ground allspice
- 2 teaspoons cream of tartar
- 1 teaspoon baking soda
- ½ teaspoon salt

SPICED SUGAR
- 1/3 cup sugar
- 1 teaspoon ground cinnamon
- ¾ teaspoon ground ginger
- ¼ teaspoon ground nutmeg
- ¼ teaspoon ground allspice

DIRECTIONS
1. In a large bowl, cream butter and sugar until light and fluffy.

2. Beat in eggs and vanilla.

3. In another bowl, whisk together the flour, spices, cream of tartar, baking soda and salt.

4. Gradually beat dry ingredients into creamed mixture.

5.   Divide dough in half; shape each into an 8-inch-long roll.

6.   Wrap in plastic; refrigerate 2 hours or until firm.

7.   Preheat oven to 350° F.

8.   In a small bowl, mix spiced sugar ingredients.

9.   Unwrap and cut dough crosswise into ¼-inch slices.

10. Press cookies into sugar mixture to coat both sides or sprinkle sugar mixture over cookies.

11. Place 2 inches apart on greased baking sheets.

12. Bake 7-9 minutes or until edges are light brown.

13. Cool on pans for 2 minutes; then, remove to wire racks to cool.

RECIPE TIPS

Freezing Instructions

- Freeze the wrapped 8-inch rolls in a resealable plastic freezer bag. Label and date. They can be kept frozen for up to three months.

- When ready to bake, unwrap frozen rolls and cut into slices. If necessary, let dough stand a few minutes at room temperature before cutting.

- Bake as directed.

SNOWBALL
CHOCOLATE SURPRISE COOKIES

Snowball Cookies are a holiday favorite (See Pecan Sandies Recipe) so we thought we would add an extra treat for you with this delightful variation. Inside these snowballs is a sweet chocolate surprise – luscious bites of Heaven.

24 Cookies – 166 calories each

INGREDIENTS

- 1 cup (2 sticks) butter, softened
- ½ cups powdered sugar
- 2 cups all-purpose flour
- 1 teaspoon pure vanilla extract
- 1 cup walnuts, very finely chopped
- ½ teaspoon salt
- 2 tablespoon water
- 24 Hershey's Chocolate Kisses, unwrapped
- **1 cup powdered sugar for dusting baked cookies**

DIRECTIONS

1. *Preheat oven to 325° F.*

2. *Line two baking sheets with parchment.*

3. *Finely chop the walnuts.*

4. *In a large bowl using an electric hand-held mixer, cream together butter and ½ cup powdered sugar until light and fluffy.*

5. *Stir in the flour, salt, vanilla, nuts, and water.*

6. *Using a 1 tablespoon cookie scoop, mold cookie dough around each chocolate kiss and roll into a ball.*

7. *Chill in the refrigerator for 1 hour.*

8. *Place on prepared baking sheets and bake for 20 to 25 minutes (Cookies should look dry with no browning.)*

9. *Cool cookies for 20 minutes,*

10. *Roll in remaining 1 cup powdered sugar.*

SOFT PUMPKIN COOKIES WITH GLAZE

These cookies are an out-of-the-ordinary, wonderful after school treat with a big glass of milk – or with your afternoon break with a fresh cup of hot coffee.

24 cookies - 228 calories each

INGREDIENTS

Cookies

- 2½ cups all-purpose flour
- 1 teaspoon baking soda
- 1 teaspoon baking powder
- 1 teaspoon ground cinnamon
- ½ teaspoon ground nutmeg
- ½ teaspoon salt
- 1½ cups granulated sugar
- ½ cup butter (1 stick), softened
- 1 cup LIBBY'S® 100% Pure Pumpkin
- 1 large egg
- 1 teaspoon vanilla extract

Glaze

- 2 cups sifted powdered sugar
- 3 tablespoons milk
- 1 tablespoon melted butter
- 1 teaspoon pure vanilla extract

DIRECTIONS

1. *Preheat oven to 350° F.*

2. *Grease baking sheets with butter or shortening.*

3. *In a medium bowl, whisk together the flour, baking soda, baking powder, cinnamon, nutmeg, and salt.*

4. In a large bowl, using a hand-held electric mixer, beat sugar and butter until well blended.

5. Beat in pumpkin, egg, and vanilla extract until smooth.

6. Slowly beat in the flour mixture.

7. Using a cookie scoop, drop onto prepared baking sheets.

8. Bake in preheated oven for 15 to 18 minutes or until edges are firm.

9. Cool on baking sheets for 2 minutes; remove to wire racks covered with paper towels to cool completely.

10. Drizzle Glaze over cookies.

Make the Glaze

1. Mix all ingredients in a small bowl until well-blended and smooth.

2. Drizzle over the completely cooled cookies.

TRIPLE CHOCOLATE CHIP COOKIES

Chocolate Chip Cookies, a favorite treat for all ages. They are also one of the easiest desserts to make and so delicious served warm from the oven. Plus, they freeze well to be used later for lunchboxes and after-school snacks. I hope you enjoy my version of this traditional American treat.

60 cookies – 126 calories each

INGREDIENTS

- 2¼ cups all-purpose flour
- 1 teaspoon baking soda
- ½ teaspoon salt
- 1 cup real butter (2 cubes), softened
- 1 cup light brown sugar, firmly packed
- ¾ cup sugar
- 2 large eggs
- 1 teaspoon vanilla extract
- 3 small packages (6 ounces) chocolate chips
  (1 semisweet; 1 milk chocolate; 1 white chocolate)
- 1 cup pecans (coarsely chopped)

DIRECTIONS

1. *Preheat oven to 375° F.*

2. *Set out two large ungreased cookie sheets.*

3. *Sift the flour, baking powder, and salt in a large bowl and set aside.*

4. *Cream together the two sugars and butter with an electric hand-held mixer set on high speed until light and fluffy.*

5. *Add eggs one at a time, mixing well after each addition; then, stir in the vanilla.*

6. *Add the dry ingredients 1/3 portion at a time, mixing well after each addition.*

7. *Stir in the three packages of chocolate chips and the nuts.*

8. Drop the dough by rounded tablespoonful onto cookie sheets. Leave about 2" between cookies.

9. Bake 10-11 minutes or until lightly browned. DO NOT OVERCOOK!

10. Let cookie stand on the baking sheet for about a minute, then carefully transfer them with a large spatula to a wire rack covered with a paper towel to cool.

RECIPE TIPS

- Cookies will keep in an airtight container for a week to 10 days.

- Frozen in an airtight container, they will keep for up to 6 months - Always thaw at room temperature

- For a slightly different flavor and texture, add ¼ cup shredded unsweetened coconut with the chips and nuts.

- Experiment with different combinations of chocolate chip flavors.

WHITE CHOCOLATE MACADAMIA NUT COOKIES

This is a different twist on the traditional chocolate chip cookie. The white chocolate and Macadamia Nuts blend deliciously with the sweet, buttery cookies.

54 cookies – 70 calories each

INGREDIENTS

- ½ cup butter, softened
- 2/3 cup sugar
- 1 large egg
- 1 teaspoon vanilla extract
- 1 cup plus 2 tablespoons all-purpose flour
- ½ teaspoon baking soda
- 1 cup macadamia nuts, finely chopped
- 1 cup white chocolate morsels

DIRECTIONS

1. Preheat oven to 350° F.

2. In a large bowl, cream butter and sugar until light and fluffy.

3. Beat in egg and vanilla.

4. In a second bowl, whisk together the flour and baking soda.

5. Gradually beat the dry ingredients into the creamed mixture.

6. Stir in nuts and baking chips.

7. Drop by heaping teaspoonfuls onto an ungreased baking sheet – about 2 inches apart.

8. Bake 10-12 minutes or until golden brown.

9. Cool on pans 1 minute – then, transfer to wire racks to cool completely.

RECIPE TIPS

Freezing Instructions

- *In freezer containers that can be tightly sealed, layer the cooled cookies between waxed paper. Freeze for up to three months.*

- *Thaw before serving.*

- *Or – if you prefer warm cookies, reheat on a baking sheet in preheated 350° oven for 3-4 minutes.*

BROWNIES, BARS & SQUARES

BAKED PEANUT BUTTER S'MORES BARS

For everyone who loves S'mores – this is a special treat. Chocolate, peanut butter, and marshmallow sandwiched between two layers of a graham cookie crust. S'MORES in dessert bar form is a delightful, prepare-ahead, summer treat.

INGREDIENTS

- ½ cup butter
- ½ cup granulated sugar
- ¼ cup packed brown sugar
- 1 egg
- 1 teaspoon vanilla
- 1 teaspoon baking powder
- 1¼ cup flour
- 1 teaspoon salt
- 6 graham crackers, finely crushed
- ½ cup peanut butter (optional)
- 2 chocolate bars (the extra big, extra-thick size, 4-ounces each)
- 1 jar of marshmallow crème (7 ounces)

DIRECTIONS

1. Preheat the oven to 350° F.

2. Line an 8 X 8-inch baking dish with parchment paper.

3. Cream together the butter and both sugars.

4. Mix in the egg and vanilla.

5. Stir in the flour, baking powder, and salt.

6. Stir in the graham cracker crumbs.

7. Press ½ of the dough into the bottom of the pan that is lined with parchment.

8. Lift out the parchment with the dough on it; set aside (this is the top cookie layer).

9. Line the pan again with parchment and press the remaining dough into the bottom of the pan.

10.   Add the next layers – Chocolate bars; Peanut Butter (optional); Marshmallow Crème; and finally, the top cookie layer.

11.   Bake for 30 minutes or until golden brown on top.

12.   Let cool completely for best serving results.

RECIPE TIPS

- Chill in the fridge overnight to allow for cleaner cuts. The bars hold together much better during the cutting process when chilled first.

- After cutting, allow to cool to room temperature to allow the marshmallow to get nice and gooey. Messy, but tasty.

- If you choose to use the peanut butter, melting it first will make it easier to spread over the chocolate. Both creamy and crunchy are delicious.

CHOCOLATE COCONUT
BUTTERSCOTCH BROWNIES

This unusual brownie comes from Tina Casaceli's Milk & Cookies: 89 Heirloom Recipes from New York's Milk & Cookies Bakery (Chronicle Books). It is a combination of flavors and textures that will not soon be forgotten.

24 bars – 401 calories each

INGREDIENTS

- 3 cups graham cracker crumbs
- 2 cups (4 sticks) unsalted butter, cut into pieces
- 1 sweetened condensed milk (14 oz)
- 2½ cups semisweet chocolate chips (16 oz)
- 2½ cups butterscotch chips (16 oz)
- 1½ cups chopped walnuts
- 2 cups sweetened coconut flakes (8 oz)

DIRECTIONS

1. Preheat the oven to 350° F.

2. Crushed the graham crackers and place in a mixing bowl; set aside.

3. Carefully melt the butter in the microwave – DO NOT OVERCOOK.

4. Immediately pour the melted butter over the graham cracker crumbs and stir until well combined.

5. Press the graham cracker mixture into the bottom of a jelly-roll pan (17¼ X 11½ by 1 inch) – be sure the layer is as even as possible.

6. Pour the condensed milk over the graham cracker crust, smoothing it out with a spatula.

7. Spread the chocolate chips evenly over the condensed milk.

8. Then, spread an even layer of butterscotch chips over the chocolate.

9. Sprinkle walnuts and coconut evenly over the top.

10. Bake in the preheated oven for about 12 minutes, or until the chocolate and butterscotch chips have melted and the coconut is lightly browned.

11. Remove from the oven and place the pan on a wire rack to cool.

12. Allow to cool completely before cutting into squares, use a serrated knife to cut into small bars or 2-inch squares.

13. Store in an airtight container – layers separated by wax paper – at room temperature for up to a week.

Chocolate Chip Oatmeal Squares

This is a yummy dessert, especially loved by teenagers. The recipe was given to me over 40 years ago by my daughter's piano teacher. It is excellent when cut in squares and eaten like a brownie, or served warm, topped with ice cream for a full-blown dessert.

18 squares – 453 calories each

INGREDIENTS

Oatmeal Bars

- 1 cup butter (2 cubes), softened
- 2 cups brown sugar (packed)
- 2 large eggs
- 2 teaspoons vanilla extract
- 2½ cups flour
- 1 teaspoon baking soda
- 1 teaspoon salt
- 3 cups Quaker® Quick Oats

Chocolate Mixture

- 12 ounces chocolate chips (large package)
- 14 ounces sweetened condensed milk (1 can)
  (Eagle Brand® is recommended)
- 2 teaspoon butter
- ½ teaspoon salt
- 2 teaspoons vanilla extract

DIRECTIONS

1. Preheat oven to 375 º F.

2. Have all ingredients at room temperature.

Make the Chocolate Mixture

3. Place all the ingredients for the chocolate mixture in a small saucepan and mix thoroughly.

4. Set over low heat so that it can melt slowly as you prepare the oatmeal bars – stir occasionally.

Make the Oatmeal Bars

5. Sift the flour, baking soda, and salt together in a small bowl and set aside.

6. Measure out the oatmeal and set aside.

7. Place the softened butter and brown sugar in a large mixing bowl. Using an electric hand-held mixer, cream the ingredients together until light and fluffy.

8. Add 1 egg at a time, mixing well after each addition – and stir in the vanilla.

9. Mix in the dry ingredients and then the oatmeal. (The dough will be stiff.)

10. Spread 2/3 of the oatmeal dough on a non-stick cookie sheet with high sides.

11. Spread melted chocolate mixture evenly across the top of the oatmeal dough.

12. Place the remaining oatmeal dough over the top. (You will have to gently flatten pieces of the dough with your hands to make it lay flat. Some of the chocolate mixture will show through.)

13. Bake for 25 minutes.

CREAM CHEESE CHOCOLATE NUT BROWNIES

Brownies have been popular for years, but when they are filled with nuts and layered with sweet cream cheese frosting, you have the ideal snack for your late afternoon treat or the perfect church potluck dessert bonanza . . . and soooooo easy to make. Bet you can't eat just one.

15 brownies – 503 calories each

INGREDIENTS

- 1¼ cups (2½ cubes) plus 1 tablespoon unsalted butter, at room temperature
- 3 (4 oz) packages Philadelphia® cream cheese, at room temperature
- 2¼ cups granulated sugar
- 1½ cups all-purpose flour, plus 2 tablespoons
- 6 large eggs
- 3 teaspoons pure vanilla extract
- ½ teaspoon baking powder
- ¼ teaspoon regular salt
- 8 ounces German chocolate, melted
- ½ cup chopped pecans, toasted

DIRECTIONS

1. *Preheat the oven to 350° F.*

2. *Coat a 9 X 13 baking pan with 1 tablespoon of butter.*

3. *With a hand-held electric mixer on medium speed, beat the cream cheese until light and fluffy, ~3 minutes – scraping the bowl as necessary.*

4. *Gradually add ½ cup of the sugar and 2 tablespoons of the flour, beating until blended.*

5. *Add 2 eggs and 1 teaspoon of the vanilla and beat until smooth; set the cream cheese batter aside.*

6. In a medium bowl, whisk together the remaining 1½ cups of flour, baking powder, and salt; set aside.

7. In another bowl, using the hand-held electric mixer, beat the 2½ cubes of butter on medium speed until smooth, ~2 minutes.

8. Gradually add the remaining 1¾ cups of sugar, scraping the bowl as necessary and beating until light and fluffy, ~2 minutes.

9. Add the remaining 4 eggs, 2 at a time, beating until blended.

10. Add the remaining 2 teaspoons of vanilla and the melted chocolate and beat until smooth.

11. Reduce the mixer speed to low, add the flour mixture, ½ cup at a time, to the chocolate batter, beating until blended.

12. Stir in the pecans.

13. Pour the chocolate batter into the prepared pan.

14. Carefully spread the cream cheese batter over the chocolate batter, cutting through the mixture with a fork several times to create a marbled design.

15. Bake until a wooden pick inserted into the center comes out with a few moist crumbs attached, ~30 to 35 minutes.

16. Transfer the pan of brownies to a wire rack to cool completely.

17. Cut into squares and serve.

CHOCOLATE MARBLE BROWNIES

9 brownies - 627 calories each

INGREDIENTS

Brownie Bars

- 4 ounces bittersweet baking chocolate
- ½ cup real butter (1 cube)
- 2 tablespoons unsweetened cocoa powder
- 1¼ cups sugar
- ¼ teaspoon salt
- 3 large eggs
- 1 teaspoon vanilla extract
- 1 cup all-purpose flour
- ½ teaspoon baking powder

Topping

- 2 cups Nestle® Chocolate Chips
  (1 cup semisweet and 1 cup white chocolate)

DIRECTIONS

1. *Line a 9" square baking pan with foil - be sure there is a foil overhang on the edges.*

2. *Spray the foil with non-stick butter-flavored cooking spray (or butter generously).*

3. *Combine the two cups of chocolate chips (for the topping) in a small bowl and stir to mix – set aside.*

4. *Using a food processor or blender, chop the bittersweet chocolate into small pieces.*

5. *Place the chocolate pieces, butter, and cocoa powder into a bowl and microwave on HIGH until the chocolate and butter are melted - stir to mix thoroughly.*

6. *Place the sugar and salt in a medium bowl and add the chocolate/butter mixture and blend completely.*

7. *Add the eggs one at a time to the sugar/chocolate mixture and mix well after each addition.*

8. *Stir in vanilla.*

9. Sift flour and baking powder into the mixture and stir until blended – using a rubber spatula to scrape the sides two or three times as you mix.

10. Pour the batter into the foil-lined baking pan and spread evenly.

11. Bake for 30 minutes until a toothpick inserted in the center comes out clean.

12. Remove from the oven and immediately sprinkle the chocolate chips over the brownies.

13. Return brownies to the oven for 1 minute to allow the chips to soften.

14. Remove from the oven and let sit for 1 minute.

15. Using the foil overhang as handles, lift the brownies out of the pan and place on a sturdy serving dish.

16. Swirl the chocolate chips over the top of the brownies to create a marbled effect.

17. Let cool completely and cut into squares.

RECIPE TIPS

VARIATION

Mocha Butter Cream Cakes

- Mix in a medium bowl: ½ cup butter, 1 cup powdered sugar, 1 to 2 teaspoons finely ground instant coffee, and 1 teaspoon vanilla.

- Cut the brownie squares in half and fill with the buttercream frosting - YUMMY!

CRANBERRY OATMEAL SQUARES

Cranberry squares are a tasty, nutritious after-school treat, a nice addition to the lunch box, or can be served warm with rich vanilla ice cream for a luscious dinner dessert.

9 squares - 258 calories each (Ice Cream not included)

INGREDIENTS

- 1 cup rolled oats
- ¾ cup brown sugar, firmly packed
- ½ cup flour
- ½ cup shredded coconut
- 1/3 cup real butter (no substitutes)
- 1 can whole cranberry sauce
- 1 tablespoon lemon juice
- Rich vanilla Ice cream (optional)

DIRECTIONS

1. *Preheat the oven to 350° F.*

2. *Generously butter an 8" square baking pan.*

3. *Place rolled oats, brown sugar, flour, and coconut together in a medium bowl.*

4. *Cut in the butter until crumbly.*

5. *Place half of the mixture in the buttered pan.*

6. *Spread the mixture evenly across the pan by pressing lightly.*

7. *Stir together the cranberry sauce and lemon juice until completely blended.*

8. *Pour over the mixture in the pan.*

9. *Top with remaining half of oats mixture and press down lightly to even out.*

10. *Bake ~ 40 minutes - cut into squares and serve with rich vanilla ice cream.*

CREAM-FILLED CHOCOLATE NUT BARS

These bars were originally called Nanaimo Bars, a tradition in the western Canadian province of British Columbia. The surprise cream filling makes them different from most American nut bars. ENJOY!

16 bars - 275 calories each

INGREDIENTS

Layer One
- 2 cups graham crackers, finely crushed
- 1 cup unsweetened shredded coconut
- ½ cup walnuts, chopped
- ½ cup dark chocolate chips
- ½ cup plus 1 tablespoon butter
- ¼ cup granulated sugar
- ¼ cup dark cocoa
- 1 large egg
- 1 teaspoon pure vanilla

Filling
- ½ cup butter, room temperature
- 2 cups powdered sugar
- 1 tablespoon cornstarch
- ¼ teaspoon vanilla extract
- 2 tablespoons hot water

DIRECTIONS

Prepare the Bottom Layer

1. Butter a 9 X 9 baking pan and line with parchment paper

2. In a large bowl, combine the graham cracker crumbs, coconut, walnuts, and chocolate chips.

3. Place ½ cup of the butter with the sugar and cocoa In a medium-sized saucepan over medium heat, cook and stir until butter has melted and the sugar has dissolved.

4. Allow to cool for a couple of minutes and whisk in the egg and vanilla until combined.

5. Pour the melted mixture over the crumb and nut mixture and stir until well combined.

6. Press into the prepared pan firmly and evenly; set aside.

Prepare the Filling

7. Using a hand-held electric mixer, cream the butter, powdered sugar, and cornstarch on medium to high speed until pale in color. Scrape down the sides of the bowl.

8. Add the vanilla and hot water.

9. Continue to beat on medium speed until the filling is light and fluffy.

10. Use a small offset spatula to spread the filling smoothly and evenly across the top of the graham cracker crumb base; set aside.

Prepare the Topping

11. Melt the chocolate chips and remaining 1 tablespoon of butter in the microwave – check and stir at 30-minute intervals until melted and well-mixed.

12. Pour mixture over the filling and spread evenly with the back of a spoon or a small offset spatula. Tap the pan on the countertop to help smooth the chocolate layer.

13. Place the pan in the refrigerator for at least 1 hour or until the chocolate top has set.

14. Run a small knife along the two edges of the pan that do not have parchment handles.

15. Carefully remove the dessert from the pan and cut into 16 bars - approximately 2" X 2".

CHERRY KUCHEN BARS

"Kuchen" is German for "cake, and used for many kinds of desserts. This recipe is made with cherry pie filling* but you can substitute other family favorites – apple, plum, blueberry, and peach are good choices.

32 bars - 183 calories each

INGREDIENTS

- ½ cup butter, softened
- ½ cup shortening
- 1¾ cups sugar
- 1½ teaspoons baking powder
- ½ teaspoon salt
- 3 eggs
- 1 teaspoon vanilla
- 3 cups all-purpose flour
- 1 can (21 oz.) cherry pie filling*

DIRECTIONS

Prepare the Bars

1. Preheat oven to 350° F.

2. Set out a 15×10×1-inch baking pan.

3. In a large mixing bowl beat butter and shortening with an electric mixer on medium speed for 30 seconds.

4. Add sugar, baking powder, and salt.

5. Beat on medium speed until combined, scraping sides of the bowl as needed.

6. Add vanilla and eggs (one at a time) – mix until combined.

7. Mix in as much of the flour as you can with the mixer. Using a wooden spoon, stir in any remaining flour.

8. Set aside 1½ cups of the dough.

9. Spread remaining dough in the bottom of an ungreased baking pan.

10. Bake for 12 minutes in the preheated oven.

11. Spread pie filling over crust in pan.

12. Scoop reserved dough into small mounds and place on top of pie filling.

13. Bake ~30 minutes more or until the top is lightly browned.

14. Cool in pan on a wire rack for 10 minutes.

15. Drizzle top with icing (recipe below).

16. Cool completely. Cut into bars to serve.

Prepare the Icing

17. In a small bowl stir together 1½ cups powdered sugar, ¼ teaspoon vanilla or almond extract, and enough milk (3 to 4 teaspoons) to make a smooth icing of drizzling consistency.

LEMON SQUARES

I first discovered these at a church buffet dinner. They instantly became one of my favorite desserts. I particularly loved them because they can be made from start to finish in a little over an hour. The combination of the buttery crust and the tangy sweetness of the lemon pudding is a taste delight - all the flavor of a mini-lemon pie in a little square confection.

18 Bars – 252 calories each

INGREDIENTS

Shortbread Crust
- 1 cup (2 cubes) unsalted butter, melted
- ½ cup granulated sugar
- 2 teaspoons pure vanilla extract
- ½ teaspoon salt
- 2 cups + 2 tablespoons all-purpose flour

Lemon Filling
- 2 cups granulated sugar
- 6 Tablespoons all-purpose flour
- 6 large eggs
- 1 cup lemon juice (about 4 lemons)

DIRECTIONS

1. Preheat the oven to 325° F.

2. Line the bottom and sides of a 9" X 13" glass baking dish with parchment paper (leave an overhang on the sides to lift the finished bars out – this will make cutting easier); set aside.

Make the Crust

3. Mix the melted butter, sugar, vanilla extract, and salt in a medium bowl.

4. Stir in the flour and mix until combined - the dough will be thick.

5. Press dough firmly into prepared pan – be sure it is even.

6. Bake for 18-20 minutes or until the edges are lightly browned - remove from oven.

Make the Filling

7. Sift the sugar and flour together in a large bowl.

8. Add the eggs and lemon juice – whisk until completely combined.

9. Pour filling over warm crust.

10. Bake in preheated oven for 22-25 minutes or until the center is relatively set and does not jiggle. (Give the pan a light tap with an oven mitt to test.)

11. Remove bars from the oven and cool completely at room temperature.

12. Cool on wire rack at room temperature for about 2 hours.

13. Refrigerate until well-chilled (1-2 hours). Bars are best served chilled.

To Serve

14. Using the overhand of parchment paper, carefully lift bars out of the pan and place on cutting board.

15. Sprinkle lightly with powdered sugar and cut into squares before serving.

RECIPE TIPS

- Use a glass or ceramic dish.

- Sift the flour and sugar together before adding the eggs and lemon juice to ensure that it will mix well without lumps. You can proceed without sifting, but it's better if you do.

- Use fresh lemon juice for the best flavor.

- For neat squares, wipe the knife clean between each cut.

- Cover and store leftover lemon bars in the refrigerator for up to 1 week. (Or freeze as explained below)

Freezing Instructions

1. The lemon bars can be frozen for up to 3-4 months. Cut the cooled bars (without confectioners sugar topping) into squares, then place onto a baking sheet and freeze for 1 hour.

2. Individually wrap each bar in aluminum foil or plastic wrap and place them into a large bag or freezer container to freeze.

3. Thaw in the refrigerator, then dust with confectioners sugar before serving.

To Make Half a Recipe

*   Cut ingredient amounts in half and bake in 9" X 9" glass baking dish. Makes 9 bars (3" x 3").

*   Bake at the same oven temperature – curst for 16-18 minutes and the bars for 20 minutes or until the center doesn't jiggle.

Mississippi Mud Bars

This decadent delight is great for parties! Your guests (and family) will love them!

18 bars – 576 calories each

INGREDIENTS

The Bars

- 2 cups sugar
- 1 cup real butter (2 cubes), softened
- 4 large eggs
- 1 teaspoon vanilla extract
- 1/3 cup unsweetened cocoa powder
- 1½ cups flour
- ¾ teaspoon salt
- 1 cup pecans or walnuts, chopped
- 1 package very fresh mini-marshmallows

The Chocolate Topping

- 1 cup real butter (2 cubes), softened
- ½ cup unsweetened cocoa powder
- 1 pound powdered sugar
- 1 tablespoon milk
- 1 cup pecans or walnuts, chopped

DIRECTIONS

1. Preheat oven to 350° F.

2. Generously butter and flour a 13" X 9" baking pan.

Make the Bars

3. Sift flour, cocoa, and salt together and set aside.

4. Cream sugar and butter together in a large mixing bowl until well-mixed and fluffy.

5. Add one egg at a time, mixing well after each addition - then add the vanilla.

6. *Mix in the flour mixture and stir until all ingredients are blended.*

7. *Stir in the walnuts.*

8. *Pour in the prepared pan and bake for 35 minutes or until a toothpick inserted in the center comes out clean.*

9. *Cover the top with 1 package very fresh mini-marshmallows and bake for 5 minutes more until the marshmallows begin to melt slightly.*

Make the Chocolate Topping

10. *Place butter, cocoa, powdered sugar, and milk in a medium saucepan and heat stirring constantly until butter melts and the mixture thickens to a hot frosting consistency.*

11. *Drizzle over the top of the bars and sprinkle with the chopped nuts.*

OLD-FASHIONED APPLE PIE SQUARES

Think you need a knife and fork to dig into a slice of apple pie? Think again! This delightful recipe turns America's Apple Pie into a quick grab-and-go pick-me-up. Great for after school snacks or yummy treats for the office, that will earn you a round of applause.

16 bars - 330 calories each

INGREDIENTS

- 3 cups, plus 2 tablespoons flour, divided
- 1 teaspoon salt1¼ cups (2½ sticks) butter, chilled and cubed
- 1 large egg, lightly beaten
- 5 tablespoons water
- 1 tablespoon white vinegar
- 6 cups sliced baking apples (~4 medium), peeled, cored, and sliced
- 1½ cups granulated sugar
- ½ teaspoon cinnamon
- 2 tablespoons flour
- 4 tablespoons tapioca
- 2 tablespoons milk
- Powdered sugar (optional)

DIRECTIONS

Make the Crust

1. In a large mixing bowl, combine 3 cups flour with salt.

2. With a fork or a pastry blender, press butter into flour mixture until it resembles small crumbs; set aside.

3. In a small bowl, whisk together the egg, water, and vinegar.

4. Pour into the flour mixture and stir until all is moistened and a loose dough is formed. Shape the dough into two equal-sized balls.

5. Preheat oven to 425° F.

6. On a clean, floured surface, roll out half the dough to fit a 10 X 15-inch baking sheet, leaving a ½" border on the sides.

7. Place dough on a baking sheet.

Make the Filling

8. In a medium bowl, combine apples, sugar, cinnamon, the remaining 2 tablespoons flour, and tapioca – mix until completely blended.

9. Place the apples over the dough on the baking sheet in an even layer.

10. Roll out remaining dough and cover apple slices.

11. Brush top of the dough with milk. Bake 10 minutes.

12. Lower heat to 375° F. and bake an additional 25 minutes.

13. Cool completely, and trim outer 1/2 inch of crust from all sides.

14. Cut remaining pie into bars, and sprinkle with sifted powdered sugar if desired.

RECIPE TIPS

- If pressed for time or hate making crust – use Pillsbury™ Refrigerated Pie Crust instead of making it yourself. It's not as good but will do in a pinch.

- The sugar may melt on to the sides of your baking sheet. It will look messy, but it's easy to clean up with a little soap and water.

- Used trimmed crust (crumbled) as an ice cream topping – YUM!

- For tapioca – check the baking section of your supermarket, or the pudding and gelatin shelf.

Pecan Pie Bars

My favorite treat after school was a mini pecan pie from a warm little bakery on Main Street that I passed on my way home. These bars are reminiscent of those wonderful bites of heaven. Treat yourself and your family today. ENJOY!

10 bars – 731 calories each

INGREDIENTS

The Crust

- 2 cups all-purpose flour
- 1/3 cup sugar
- ¼ teaspoon salt
- ¾ cup cold butter, cubed

The Filling

- 4 large eggs
- 1½ cups corn syrup
- 1½ cups sugar
- 3 tablespoons butter, melted
- 1½ teaspoons vanilla extract
- 2½ cups chopped pecans

DIRECTIONS

Make the Crust

1. Preheat oven to 350° F.

2. Butter a jelly-roll baking pan (15x10x1").

3. In a large bowl, whisk together the flour, sugar, and salt.

4. Cut in cold butter until mixture resembles coarse crumbs. (A pastry cutter is great for this if you have one.)

5. Press into a prepared baking pan and bake for 20 minutes.

Make the Filling

6. In a large bowl, whisk together the eggs, corn syrup, sugar, melted butter, and vanilla.

7. Stir in the pecans and spread over hot crust.

8. Bake 25-30 minutes longer or until filling is set.

9. Set on a wire rack and cool completely in pan.

10. Cut into bars.

11. Serve warm with vanilla ice cream, or room temperature whenever the craving strikes.

RAISIN NUT SQUARES
WITH ORANGE ICING

These scrumptious soft-chewy frosted raisin bars are a tasty treat at any time of the day. And . . . they are the perfect grab-and-go breakfast.

18 bars – 151 calories each

INGREDIENTS

The Raisin Bars
- 1 cup raisins
- 1½ cups water
- 2 tablespoons butter
- 2 cups flour
- 1 cup sugar
- 1 teaspoon baking powder
- 1 teaspoon baking soda
- 1 teaspoon cinnamon
- ¾ teaspoon salt
- ½ teaspoon nutmeg
- ½ cup chopped walnuts

The Icing
- 1 cup powdered sugar
- 1 tablespoon butter, melted and cooled
- 1 tablespoon water
- 1 teaspoon orange juice
- 1 teaspoon lemon juice
- ½ teaspoon lemon zest
- ½ teaspoon orange zest

DIRECTIONS

1. *Preheat oven to 350° F.*

2. *Grease and flour a 9x13" baking pan*

Make the Bars

3. In a small saucepan, simmer 1 cup raisins, 1-1/2 cups water, and 2 tablespoons butter until only one cup liquid remains. Remove from heat and cool. DO NOT DRAIN – the liquid is necessary.

4. In a medium mixing bowl, sift together flour, sugar, baking powder, baking soda, cinnamon, salt, and nutmeg.

5. Stir in chopped walnuts. Add cooled raisin mixture and stir to combine. (It will create wet cookie dough.)

6. Spread mixture out evenly in the greased pan.

7. Bake 15-20 minutes, or until the top is golden brown.

8. Remove from the oven and let cool.

Make the Frosting

1. Combine powdered sugar, butter, water, orange juice, lemon juice, lemon zest, and orange zest.

2. Mix well – until smooth and creamy.

3. Drizzle over cooled cake in pan.

4. Cut into squares and serve.

Rich Chocolate Brownies

This is an easy brownie recipe that always turns out well. Make a batch to share with your friends and neighbors. Perfect choice for parties – make smaller squares and serve more people.

30 brownies – 212 calories each

INGREDIENTS

The Brownies

- 2 cups flour - plus 2 tablespoons
- ¾ cup powdered milk
- 2 cups sugar
- ½ cup unsweetened cocoa
- ¾ teaspoon baking powder
- ¼ teaspoon salt, plus 1/8 teaspoon salt
  (If you double the recipe, use ¾ teaspoon)
- 1½ cubes butter (no substitutes)
- 3 large eggs
- 1½ teaspoon vanilla extract
- ¼ cup water (plus 2 tablespoons)
  (If you double the recipe, use ¾ cup)
- 1 cup chopped nuts - walnuts or pecans (optional)

The Frosting (for a single batch)

- 1 cube butter
- 2 tablespoon unsweetened cocoa
- 1 dash salt
- 1 teaspoon vanilla extract
- 2 cups powdered sugar (heaping cups)
- 2 to 3 tablespoons evaporated milk
  (Enough milk to reach desired consistency)

DIRECTIONS

Make the Brownies

1. Preheat the oven to 300° F.

2. Lightly butter an 11" X 17" cookie sheet with high sides.

3. Mix all dry ingredients in a large bowl.

4. In a separate bowl, mix butter, eggs, vanilla, and water until smooth.

5. Pour egg mixture into dry ingredients and mix thoroughly – then stir in the nuts, if using.

6. Pour into the baking pan and spread evenly.

7. Bake for 20 minutes or until a toothpick inserted in the center comes out clean.

8. The recipe can be doubled if you need a large batch for school treats or church potluck.

Make the Frosting

9. Melt butter in a saucepan - remove from heat.

10. Add cocoa and stir well.

11. Add a dash of salt, vanilla, and powdered sugar.

12. An electric hand mixer works best - but can be mixed with a wooden spoon.

13. Slowly add evaporated milk while beating - until it reaches a good spreading consistency that will hold its shape.

RECIPE TIPS

- This recipe works best when baked in an 11" X 17" cookie pan with high sides - worth the investment if you don't already have one.

- The frosting recipe that is included is a great standard chocolate frosting for any cake.

SALTED CARAMEL
CHOCOLATE CHIP COOKIE BARS

These amazing Salted Caramel Chocolate Chip Cookie Bars, with gooey caramel centers, are so incredible, everyone will be asking for the recipe.

24 bars - 311 calories each

INGREDIENTS

- 1 cup unsalted butter, softened
- 1 cup packed light brown sugar
- ½ cup granulated sugar
- 2 large eggs
- 1 teaspoon vanilla extract
- 1 teaspoon kosher salt
- 1 teaspoon baking soda
- 2½ cups all-purpose flour
- 2 cups semisweet chocolate chips
- 1 can (14 ounces) sweetened condensed milk
- 10 ounces soft caramels, *unwrapped*
- 1 teaspoon flaked sea salt

DIRECTIONS

1. *Preheat the oven to 350° F.*

2. *Line a 9 x 13 baking dish with foil and spray liberally with nonstick cooking spray.*

3. *In a medium bowl with a hand-held electric mixer, beat the softened butter with both sugars until light and fluffy, ~2 minutes.*

4. *Add the eggs, vanilla, salt, and baking soda.*

5. *Mix well, scraping down the sides of the bowl with a spatula, as needed.*

6. *Turn the speed to low and add the flour ½ cup at a time.*

7. *Beat to combine, then stir in the chocolate chips with a wooden spoon.*

8. Press half of the cookie dough into the bottom of the prepared baking dish.

9. In a medium saucepan, mix the sweetened condensed milk and unwrapped caramels.

10. Set over medium-low heat and stir until the caramels melt and the mixture is smooth and creamy.

11. Pour the caramel sauce over the cookie dough base.

12. Drop the remaining cookie dough over the caramel sauce in small teaspoons-sized clumps. Bake the bars for 25-30 minutes, until the center is just set.

13. Remove from the oven and immediately sprinkle with sea salt flakes.

14. Allow the bars to cool completely.

15. Then lift the bars out of the pan by the edges of the foil and cut into squares

16. Store in an airtight container at room temperature for up to 3 days.

RECIPE TIPS

- The bars can be frozen, but wrap well to prevent freezer burn – date and label.

- Thaw and warm to room temperature before serving.

SALTED DOUBLE CHOCOLATE CHIP SKILLET COOKIE

Have fun with this variation of America's Favorite – Chocolate Chip Cookie – for Two. BTW, this is made in a cast-iron skillet, which will be a great addition to your kitchen.

2 servings of the cookie - 312 calories each (add extra calories for ice cream)

INGREDIENTS
- ½ cup butter (1 cube), melted
- ½ cup brown sugar, packed
- ¼ cup turbinado (raw) sugar
- 1 teaspoon vanilla
- 1¼ cup flour
- ½ teaspoon baking soda
- ½ teaspoon salt
- 2 ounces milk chocolate, finely chopped
- ½ cup dark chocolate chips
- Vanilla ice cream
- Salt Flakes (optional)
- Extra chocolate shavings

DIRECTIONS
1. Heat oven to 350° F.

2. With a handheld electric mixer, combine the melted butter and both sugars.

3. Beat in the egg and vanilla.

4. Add the flour, baking soda, and salt to the mixture.

5. Stir until all ingredients are well mixed.

6. Stir in both chocolates until well-mixed – scraping down the sides with a spatula.

7. Press the dough into a lightly buttered 8"-10" cast-iron skillet.

8. Bake until center is firm, but still a little gooey, ~18-20 minutes.

9. Remove and sprinkle lightly with flakey sea salt.

10. Let cool for a few minutes.

11. Top with vanilla ice cream and enjoy it with your best friend!

Toffee Shortbread

Surprise and delight yourself and everyone you know with these amazing shortbread bars.
They can be made with or without chocolate chips – delicious either way.

30 bars - 242 calories each (with chocolate/butterscotch chips)

INGREDIENTS

- 2 1/3 cups all-purpose flour
- 2/3 cup rice flour
- ½ teaspoon table salt
- 1½ cups (3 cubes) unsalted butter, room temperature
- 6 tablespoons super-fine sugar
- 6 tablespoons packed light brown sugar
- ¾ cup mini chocolate chips or butterscotch chips
- ¾ cup toffee bits, such as HEATH or SKOR

DIRECTIONS

1. Preheat the oven to 325° F.

2. Grease the bottom and sides of a 9 x 13-inch metal baking pan. (If using a glass baking dish, lower the oven temperature by 25 degrees.)

3. Line the pan with parchment paper, leaving a 1-inch overhang on each side to allow for easy removal.

4. Sift or whisk the all-purpose flour, rice flour, and salt together; set aside.

5. Using an electric hand-held mixer, beat butter on medium speed until smooth, ~ 2 minutes.

6. Add sugars and cream together with the butter until light and fluffy (almost like whipped cream), ~2-3 minutes more.

7. Using a wooden spoon, fold the flour mixture into the butter mixture, ½ cup at a time – continue to mix until well-blended.

8.   Add the chocolate chips and toffee bits and stir until they are evenly mixed throughout the dough.

9.   Scoop the dough into the prepared pan and press firmly to distribute it evenly. (Work quickly so the warmth of your hands doesn't melt the butter.)

10.   Use the back of a spoon to smooth the surface.

11.   Prick the dough all over with a fork.

12.   Bake in the preheated oven for 45 minutes.

13.   Remove from the oven and prick again to release any trapped air.

14.   Bake for an additional 10 to 20 minutes depending on your preference — less baking time yields a tender, crumbly cookie; more time yields a firmer result.

15.   Cool in the pan on a wire rack for 7 to 8 minutes.

16.   Cut into ¾" to 1" wide rectangles. This is easily done with a sharp knife, slicing the shortbread lengthwise into three even sections, wiping the knife clean after each cut.

17.   Rotate the pan 180° and continue cutting the shortbread crosswise into ¾" to 1" rectangles. You can stop at that point (30 bars), or you can cut them in half again for 60 bars.

18.   Leve the cookies in the pan to cool completely.

19.   Carefully remove the shortbread to a cutting board by lifting them out with the parchment paper overhangs. A large spatula gives good additional support.

20.   You may need to re-slice the pieces to separate them.

21.   Store in an airtight container in a dark place.

THE HOLIDAY
COLLECTION

CLASSIC SHORTBREAD COOKIES

Classic Shortbread Cookies are made with only three ingredients. They are mouthwatering, buttery, and melt-in-your-mouth delicious. This is a classic holiday cookie, made two ways!

36 cookies – 118 calories each

INGREDIENTS

- 1½ cups (3 cubes) butter salted and softened at room temperature
- 1 cup powdered sugar
- 3 cups all-purpose flour

DIRECTIONS

1. Preheat oven to 325° F.

2. Line an ungreased cookie sheet with parchment paper – the paper should extend off the sides of the pan for easy lifting after baking.

3. Place the butter in a large bowl - using a hand-held electric mixer on medium, cream until smooth, ~30 seconds.

4. Add the sugar and continue mixing until well blended, scraping down the sides of the bowl several times.

5. Turn the mixer to low and blend in the flour until dough is soft and crumbly.

Baking Sheet Cookies

6. Scrape the dough onto the prepared cookie sheet and pat until it is level and covers the pan.

7. Bake for 12 to 15 minutes, or until just done (slightly golden). Do not let it get brown. Remove from the oven.

8. Using the overhang edges of the parchment paper as handles, lift the baked dough and cut into desired shapes – squares, circles, triangles, etc.

9. Transfer to a wire rack covered with a paper towel to finish cooling.

RECIPE TIPS

- *If you use salted butter, don't add salt to the recipe. With unsalted butter, add ¼ teaspoon salt to the recipe.*

To Use Cookie Cutters

- *After you have mixed the ingredients (completing Step #5 above), scoop the dough onto a lightly floured board and roll it out to ¼ inch thickness; or knead it just until the dough comes together (do not overwork) and then, roll out to ¼ inch thickness.*

- *Cut into desired shapes and place on the parchment-covered baking sheet and bake as directed above.*

- *You can split the dough in half – use one half for a sheet cookie that you cut into shapes; and roll out the second half for cutting into desired shapes with cookie cutters.*

Freezing Instructions

- *Freeze cookies in an airtight container and place for up to 3 months – be sure to date and label the container.*

CRUSHED PEPPERMINT MELTIES

Do you need a lovely Christmas gift for neighbors? These festive peppermint cookies that melt in your mouth are perfect when wrapped in red or green plastic wrap and topped with a bright holiday bow. They will also disappear quickly when served to family and friends.

30 cookies – 126 calories each

INGREDIENTS
Cookies
- 1 cup butter, softened
- ½ cup confectioners sugar
- ½ teaspoon peppermint extract
- 1¼ cups all-purpose flour
- ½ cup cornstarch

Frosting
- 2 tablespoons butter, softened
- 2 tablespoons 2% milk
- ¼ teaspoon peppermint extract
- 2 to 3 drops red food coloring (optional)
- 1½ cups confectioners sugar
- ½ cup crushed peppermint candies

DIRECTIONS
Make the Cookies
1. Place butter and powdered sugar in a small bowl and beat with a hand-held electric mixer until light and fluffy – then, mix in the extract.

2. Place flour and cornstarch in another small bowl and whisk together until thoroughly mixed.

3. Gradually add the flour mixture to the creamed ingredients and beat until well-combined.

4. Cover and refrigerate for 30 minutes or until firm enough to handle.

5. Preheat oven to 350° F.

6. Set out ungreased baking sheets.

7. When the dough is chilled, shape into 1" balls; place 2 inches apart on baking sheets.

8. Bake 9 to 11 minutes or until bottoms are light brown.

9. Transfer cookies to wire racks to cool completely.

Make the Frosting

1. In a small bowl, cream the butter with an electric mixer.

2. Add the milk, extract and food coloring (if desired) – mix well. (I prefer white frosting, it sets off the peppermint candy nicely.)

3. Gradually mix in the powdered sugar until smooth.

4. Spread over well-cooled cookies; sprinkle with crushed candies.

5. Store in an airtight container.

EASY SPRINKLE COOKIES

The child in all of us loves sprinkles – especially when they are sprinkled on soft, sweet sugar cookies. This recipe is so easy to make that you will want to use it during the holidays for every child you know and love (including yourself). You can change the sprinkle colors to match every holiday or just for fun.

36 Cookies – 92 calories each

INGREDIENTS

- 2½ cups flour
- 1 teaspoon baking powder
- ¼ teaspoon baking soda
- ½ teaspoon salt
- 1 cup unsalted butter, softened (not melted)
- 1¼ cups sugar
- 2 oz cream cheese, softened
- 1 large egg
- 1 teaspoon vanilla
- ½ teaspoon almond extract
- ¾ - 1 cup sprinkles (nonpareils, jimmies or colored sugar sprinkles)

DIRECTIONS

1. *Preheat oven to 350° F.*

2. *Line baking sheets with parchment paper.*

3. *Place sprinkles in a small mixing bowl; set aside.*

4. *Whisk together flour, baking powder, baking soda, and salt; set aside.*

5. *Using a hand-held electric mixer – blend butter, sugar, and cream cheese.*

6. *Mix in egg, vanilla, and almond extracts.*

7. *Stir in the flour mixture and continue to stir until well combined. (If you live in a very humid climate, you may need to chill dough for at least 30 minutes or it may be too sticky to create the cookie balls.)*

8.   *Scoop dough out 1½ tablespoons at a time – a cookie scoop works well for this.*

9.   *Shape the dough into balls and roll in the sprinkles.*

10.   *Place on a prepared baking sheet about 2-inches apart.*

11.   *With the bottom of a cup or glass, flatten cookies about halfway.*

12.   *Bake one sheet at a time in the preheated oven, about 9 minutes (cookies should appear slightly under-baked).*

13.   *Cool slightly on the baking sheet and transfer to a wire rack to cool completely.*

14.   *Store cookies in an airtight container.*

GINGERBREAD COOKIES

This Gingerbread Cookie recipe makes perfectly soft and chewy cookies and with just the right amount of spices and rich molasses flavor. The dough is easy to work with and they are fun to decorate. These will quickly become a new favorite holiday cookie!

24 cookies – 229 calories each

INGREDIENTS

Cookies

- 3 cups flour
- 1 tablespoon ground ginger
- 2 teaspoons ground cinnamon
- ¼ teaspoon ground cloves
- ¼ teaspoon ground nutmeg
- ¾ teaspoon baking powder
- ½ teaspoon baking soda
- ½ teaspoon salt
- ¾ cup packed dark brown sugar
- 10 tablespoons unsalted butter, softened
- 1 egg yolk (large)
- 1½ teaspoons vanilla extract
- ½ cup molasses (not blackstrap)
- 1 - 2 tablespoons milk

Royal Icing

- 4 cups powdered sugar
- 3 tablespoons meringue powder (must have)
- 9 to 10 tablespoons water (room temperature
- Gel food coloring (when using for other decorating other cookies)
- ¼ teaspoon vanilla extract

DIRECTIONS

1.   *Preheat oven to 350° F.*

Make the Cookies

2.   *In a mixing bowl whisk together flour, ginger, cinnamon, cloves, nutmeg, baking powder, baking soda, and salt; set aside.*

3.   *Using a hand-held electric mixer, cream sugar and butter until well combined. Be sure to stop and scrape down the sides of the bowl occasionally.*

4.   *Add the egg yolk, vanilla, molasses, and 1 tablespoon milk.*

5.   *With the mixer on low speed, slowly add dry ingredients and mix until combined. Add just enough additional milk as needed to hold the dough together.*

6.   *Divide dough into two equal portions.*

7.   *Place dough between two sheets of parchment paper and roll out each portion evenly to ¼-inch thickness (preferably into an oblong or rectangular shape so it will fit on a cookie sheet).*

8.   *Place the cookie sheet in the freezer 10 - 20 minutes to chill.*

9.   *When the dough is firm, cut into shapes with cookie cutters.*

10.   *Remove each cookie from paper using a thin metal spatula or pastry scraper, if needed.*

11.   *Transfer to parchment paper-lined cookie sheet, spacing cookies about 1-inch apart.*

12.   *Place powdered sugar and meringue powder in a medium mixing bowl.*

13.   *Using a hand-held electric mixer on low speed, add 4 tablespoons water and the vanilla until well-combined.*

14.   *Add more water to thin as needed and increase speed; whip mixture until it is glossy and thick.*

15.   *Separate into bowls and tint with food coloring, if desired.*

16.   *Transfer to piping bags fitted with tiny round tips or into Ziploc sandwich bags with a corner cut off.*

17.   *Decorate cookies with icing and add sprinkles if desired.*

18. Let icing set at room temperature until set and store in an airtight container.

19. Bake in preheated oven for ~8 minutes or until slightly set.

20. Remove from oven and cool on baking sheet ~2 minutes; then, transfer to a wire rack to cool completely.

21. Repeat process with remaining dough.

Make the Royal Icing (Preferred icing for decorating cookies)

1. Place all the ingredients together in a large bowl.

2. Using an electric mixer on high speed (use the whisk attachment if you have one), mix the ingredients for 1 ½ to 2 minutes.

3. The icing will be ready when you lift the whisk or beaters and the icing drizzles down and smooths out within 5 to 10 seconds.

4. Add more water if it is too thick. (If the weather is particularly dry days, you may need up to 12-14 Tablespoons water total.) If it's too thin and the frosting is runny, add a little more sifted powdered sugar.

5. The icing dries completely in about 2 hours at room temperature.

6. If you're layering royal icing onto cookies for specific designs and need it to set quickly, place cookies in the refrigerator to help speed it up.

RECIPE TIPS

- When you **test the cookies for doneness**, there should be a slight indentation when touched. For soft cookies, be careful not to over-bake. If you prefer crisp cookies, bake them a little longer.

- The cookies are softer the second day, which I think makes them better.

HOLIDAY BUTTER COOKIES

These buttery sugar cookies are easy to roll out and have a tender/crisp texture. They are the perfect choice for any kind of cutout cookies, for any occasion. That means they do not have to be saved only for Christmas.

60 cookies – 80 calories each

INGREDIENTS
Cookies
- 1¼ cups confectioners sugar
- 1 cup + 2 tablespoons salted butter, room temperature
- 1 large egg yolk
- ½ teaspoon salt
- 2 teaspoons vanilla extract, or flavor of your choice (see "tips," below)
- 2¾ cups all-Purpose Flour

Icing
- 2¼ cups powdered sugar
- 2 tablespoons light corn syrup
- 1½ to 2 tablespoons – add more, as needed to make a pourable/spreadable icing
- Food coloring (optional)
- 1 cup coarse sugar or colored sugar for decorating (optional)

DIRECTIONS
Make the Cookies
1. *Preheat the oven to 350° F.*

2. *Lined ungreased cookie sheets with parchment paper.*

3. *Place the sugar, butter, egg yolk, salt, and extract in a medium bowl and mix with an electric mixer on medium until smooth.*

4. *Add the flour gradually - mixing until smooth. (It may seem dry at first, but will suddenly come together; If needed slowly add a tablespoon of water.)*

5.	Divide the dough in half, shape each half into a flattened disk, and wrap in plastic.

6.	Refrigerate for 2 hours, or overnight.

7.	To bake - remove the dough from the refrigerator, and let it soften for 20 to 30 minutes until it is soft enough to roll out. It may still feel cold, but it must be pliable.

8.	Work with one piece of dough at a time.

9.	Place it on a lightly floured board and use a lightly floured rolling pin.

10.	Roll out the dough to 1/8" to 3/16" thick.

11.	Cut to desired shapes with cookie cutters.

12.	Place the cookies on ungreased or parchment-lined baking sheets. The cookies do not spread, so they can be placed close together.

13.	The scraps can be gathered, re-rolled, cut, and baked.

14.	Bake the cookies for 12 to 14 minutes, until set and barely brown around the edges.

15.	Remove from the oven, and cool right on the pan. (If you've used parchment, you can lift cookies and parchment off the pan, so you can use the pan again for the next batch as the cookies cool.

16.	Repeat the process with the remaining dough, rolling, cutting, and baking.

17.	Spread with icing and decorate only completely cooled cookies

Make the Icing

1. Combine the sugar, milk, and corn syrup to make a soft, spreadable icing, adding more milk if necessary. Tint the icing with food color as desired.

2. Spread icing on the cookies, using a knife, a spoon, or your finger to spread it to the edges.

3. Sprinkle with colored sugar or other sugar decorations, as desired. Allow the icing to harden before storing the cookies.

RECIPE TIPS

- If you use unsalted butter, increase the amount of salt in the recipe to 1 teaspoon.

- **Alternate Flavoring**: Try the standard, 2 teaspoons vanilla extract, or 1 teaspoon almond extract, or a combination. For extra-strong flavors (eggnog, butter rum, etc.), start with 1/8 teaspoon, and flavor to taste.

- **To top cookies with colored sugar before baking** (no icing necessary). Reserve the egg white from the yolk you use in the dough. Mix the white with one tablespoon water. Lightly paint the cookies with the egg white/water, sprinkle with colored sugar, and bake.

- The icing should be a little on the thick side, and it won't be perfectly smooth when you apply it. But, it should settle into a smooth surface within half a minute or so. Test it by frosting one cookie and set it aside for a minute. If the glaze settles into a smooth surface, it's the right consistency. If not, add a little liquid.

- Keep in mind – it's easier to add more liquid than to stir in more sugar, so start with icing that is thicker than you think it should be, then add milk little by little to get the consistency right.

PEANUT BUTTER BLOSSOMS

Soft peanut butter cookies with a chocolate kiss in the center – what more can you ask for? Everyone LOVES these peanut butter cookies! They are easy-peasy to make and will disappear quickly.

30 Cookies – 143 Calories each

INGREDIENTS

- 1¾ cups all-purpose flour
- 1 teaspoon baking soda
- ½ teaspoon salt
- ½ cup unsalted butter, at room temperature
- ½ cup creamy peanut butter
- ½ cup granulated sugar
- ½ cup packed light brown sugar
- 1 large egg
- 1 tablespoon milk
- 1 teaspoon pure vanilla extract
- 30 Hershey's Chocolate Kisses, unwrapped
- Extra sugar for rolling cookies before baking

DIRECTIONS

1. In a medium bowl, whisk together the flour, baking soda, and salt; set aside.

2. Using a stand mixer or hand mixer, cream together butter, peanut butter, ½ cup granulated sugar, and brown sugar until smooth and fluffy, ~5 minutes, scraping down the side of the bowl several times during the mixing process.

3. Add the egg, milk and vanilla extract. Beat until combined.

4. Add the flour mixture a little at a time and mix on low until just combined. Don't over mix.

5. Wrap the dough in plastic wrap and chill in the refrigerator for at least 30 minutes. It can be chilled for up to 72 hours.

6. Place the Hershey's Kisses in the freezer so they are frozen when you put them on the cookies. This will help the kisses to keep their shape and not melt.

7. When ready to bake, preheat oven to 350° F.

8. Line a large baking sheet with a Silpat baking mat or parchment paper.

9. Place 1/3 to ½ cup sugar in a small bowl.

10. Roll the peanut butter cookie dough into balls, a scant tablespoon of dough per cookie.

11. Roll the cookie dough balls in the sugar until they are generously coated.

12. Place the cookie dough balls onto the prepare baking sheet, ~2" apart.

13. Bake the cookies until they start to crack on the edges, 8 or 9 minutes.

14. Remove the baking sheet from the oven and lightly press a frozen chocolate kiss into the center of each cookie, allowing it to crack slightly.

15. Return to oven and bake for an additional 2 minutes.

16. Remove from the oven - cool on the baking sheet for 2 to 3 minutes.

17. Transfer to a wire rack covered with a paper towel – let cool until the kisses harden.

18. If you want to speed up the process, you can put the cookies in the freezer so the kisses will harden faster.

19. Cookies can be stored in an airtight container for up to four days (if they last that long).

RASPBERRY ALMOND SHORTBREAD THUMBPRINT COOKIES

These Raspberry Almond Shortbread Thumbprint Cookies are simply delicious and should have a place of honor on your holiday cookie tray!

36 cookies – 117 calories each

INGREDIENTS

- 2 cups + 2 tablespoons flour*
- ¼ teaspoon salt
- 1 cup unsalted butter, cold and diced into pieces
- 2/3 cup granulated sugar
- ½ teaspoon almond extract
- ½ cup seedless raspberry jam (strawberry is also tasty)

DIRECTIONS

Make the Cookies

1. Preheat oven to 350° F.

2. In a mixing bowl whisk together flour and salt, set aside.

3. Using an electric hand-held mixer, blend butter and sugar until combined (it will take a minute or two since the butter is cold) - stir in almond extract.

4. Add dry ingredients and blend until mixture comes together (the mixture will be dry and crumbly at first, continue to mix until blended).

5. Make 1-inch balls from the dough (~1 tablespoon each), and place 2-inches apart on ungreased baking sheets.

6. Make a small indentation with thumb or forefinger in each cookie (just large enough for ¼ to ½ teaspoon of jam).

7. Fill each indentation with jam.

8. Chill prepared cookies in the refrigerator for 20 minutes (or freezer for 10 minutes).

9.   Bake in preheated oven 14 - 16 minutes.

10.   Cool several minutes on the baking sheet then, transfer to a wire rack to cool.

11.   Store cookies in an airtight container until ready to serve.

RECIPE TIPS

- Scoop flour with a measuring cup and cut and then, level with a table knife.

- Do not whisk or sift first and don't spoon flour into the measuring cup.

Sugar Cookies

These cookies are soft and fluffy with just the right amount of sweetness – a family favorite for the holidays (or any time of the year). They are delicious with or without frosting and make a great freezer-friendly holiday cookie! They are yummy treats for Santa, the family, or friends.

60 small frosted cookies - 175 calories each

INGREDIENTS

Cookies

- 1½ cups powdered sugar
- 1 cup butter, softened
- 1 teaspoon vanilla
- ½ teaspoon almond extract
- 1 large egg
- 2½ cups all-purpose flour1 teaspoon baking soda
- 1 teaspoon cream of tartar

Frosting

- 3 cups powdered sugar
- 3 to 5 tablespoons milk
- ¼ teaspoon vanilla
- Food colors (optional)
- Colored sugar or candy sprinkles (as desired)

DIRECTIONS

Make the Cookies

1. *Grease cookie sheets well or line with parchment paper.*

2. *Place 1½ cups powdered sugar, softened butter, vanilla, and almond extracts, and egg in a large bowl – beat with an electric mixer on medium speed until well-blended.*

3. *Whisk together the flour, baking soda, and cream of tartar.*

4. *Gradually add the flour mixture to the creamed mixture.*

5. *Divide dough in half; shape dough into 2 disks, and wrap each one in plastic wrap. Cover and refrigerate at least 2 hours.*

6. *Preheat the oven to 375° F.*

7. *Place a disk on a lightly floured surface and roll to a 1¼ inch thickness.*

8. *Use 2" or 2½" cookie cutters of desired shapes to cut the cookies.*

9. *Place cutouts at least 2 inches apart on prepared cookie sheets.*

10. *Bake 7 to 8 minutes or until edges are light brown.*

11. *Cool 1 minute on the cookie sheet and then, transfer to wire cooling racks.*

12. *Cool completely before frosting.*

Make the Frosting

1. *Place all ingredients except food coloring and sprinkles in a medium bowl and beat with an electric mixer until frosting is smooth and spreadable.*

2. *If frosting is too stiff to spread, add additional milk, 1 teaspoon at a time.*

3. *Tint with food color, if desired.*

4. *Spread frosting on completely cooled cookies.*

5. *Decorate as desired with colored sugar or candy sprinkles.*

6. *Let stand about 4 hours or until frosting is set.*

7. *Store covered in an airtight container at room temperature with waxed paper between layers.*

ABOUT THE AUTHOR

Nancy N. Wilson

Nancy N Wilson is a writer, blogger and bestselling author of more than 30 books. She was born and reared in a small farming community in Southern Arizona. She earned a B.S. Degree in Education and Psychology at Utah State University and an MBA at Thunderbird School of Global Management.

Her one constant lifetime companion has been cooking, which began as a young child when her mother gave her free reign in the kitchen to create masterpieces of flour, sugar, spices, and anything else she could find in the cupboards.

When she finally learned to follow a recipe, Mexican food and a wide variety of desserts (including cookies) were her two favorite types of foods to prepare.

Growing up in a small town in the 50s and 60s gave her many free hours to experiment and master the craft. She especially enjoyed cooking for her friends.

Even with college, marriage and all the adventures of life, her love of cooking never faltered. She was always looking for new recipes and new creative touches for traditional dishes. She cooked her way through years of marriage, a divorce, and a multi-faceted career,

She has lived and worked on both the East Coast and West Coast of the United States, consulted with major corporations in Europe and Japan, and traveled extensively throughout Central and South America.

In 2007, she returned to Arizona to live near her two sons and to do what she has always wanted to do – WRITE.

She now spends her time contributing to her "Healthy Living Blog, (https://Mamaslegacycookbooks.com), testing new recipes, and writing and publishing non-fiction books – half of which are cookbooks.

She finds great satisfaction and joy in sharing all she has learned with you, her readers, and hopes that you will benefit and develop a passion for cooking as great or greater than hers.

Other Books by This Author

Cookbooks

Candy Making Made Easy - Instructions and 17 Starter Recipes

Cake Making Made Easy - Instructions and 60 Cakes

Cook Ahead – Freezer to Table

The Healthy Diet Cookbook

Garden Fresh Soups and Stews

Juicing for Life – The Secret to Vibrant Health

Sweet Treats – Candy, Cookies, Cake, Ice Cream, Pudding, and Pie

Fun in the Kitchen for Tweens and Teens

Single, On-Your-Own, and Hungry

Mama's Legacy Cookbook Series

Seven Volumes Available

Dinner – 55 Easy Recipes (Volume I)

Breakfast and Brunch – 60 Delicious Recipes (Volume II)

Dessert – 50 Scrumptious Recipes (Volume III)

Chicken – 25 Classic Dinners (Volume IV)

Mexican Favorites – 21 Traditional Recipes (Volume V)

Side Dishes – 60 Great Recipes (Volume VI)

Sauce Recipes – 50 Tasty Choices (Volume VII)

Health and Fitness

DETOX – The Master Cleanse Diet

Growing Tomatoes – Everything You Need to Know, and More

Stop Eating Yourself into an Early Grave

WOW! You Look Fantastic!

Business

Attitude Adjustment

Starting an Online Business

Congratulations, You Are Self-Employed

Books Written under Pseudonyms

Power Up Your Brain – Five Simple Strategies (J. J. Jackson)

Clicker Training for Dogs (Amy Ellsworth)

Making Money with Storage Unit Auctions (Bryce Cranston)

www.ingramcontent.com/pod-product-compliance
Lightning Source LLC
Chambersburg PA
CBHW081551040426
42448CB00016B/3281